Y0-DDS-257

AICPA Audit and Accounting Guide

AGRICULTURAL PRODUCERS AND AGRICULTURAL COOPERATIVES

With Conforming Changes
as of May 1, 2004

This edition of the AICPA Audit and Accounting Guide *Agricultural Producers and Agricultural Cooperatives,* which was originally issued in 1987, has been modified by the AICPA staff to include certain changes necessary because of the issuance of authoritative pronouncements since the Guide was originally issued (see page iv). The changes made in the current year are identified in a schedule in appendix E of the Guide. The changes do *not* include all those that might be considered necessary if the Guide were subjected to a comprehensive review and revision.

AMERICAN INSTITUTE OF CERTIFIED PUBLIC ACCOUNTANTS

1 2 3 4 5 6 7 8 9 0 AAP 0 9 8 7 6 5 4

ISBN 0-87051-489-X

NOTICE TO READERS

This AICPA Audit and Accounting Guide has been prepared by the AICPA Agribusiness Special Committee to assist preparers of financial statements of agricultural producers and agricultural cooperatives in preparing financial statements in conformity with generally accepted accounting principles and to assist auditors in auditing and reporting on such financial statements in accordance with generally accepted auditing standards.

Descriptions of accounting principles and financial reporting practices in Audit and Accounting Guides are approved by the affirmative vote of at least two-thirds of the members of the Accounting Standards Executive Committee, which is the senior technical body of the AICPA authorized to speak for the AICPA in the areas of financial accounting and reporting. Statement on Auditing Standards (SAS) No. 69, *The Meaning of* Present Fairly in Conformity With Generally Accepted Accounting Principles, identifies AICPA Audit and Accounting Guides that have been cleared by the Financial Accounting Standards Board (FASB) as sources of accounting principles in category *b* of the hierarchy of generally accepted accounting principles that it establishes. This Audit and Accounting Guide has been cleared by the FASB. AICPA members should consider the accounting principles described in this Audit and Accounting Guide if the accounting treatment of a transaction or event is not specified by a pronouncement covered by Rule 203 of the AICPA Code of Professional Conduct. In such circumstances, the accounting treatments specified by this Audit and Accounting Guide should be used, or the member should be prepared to justify another treatment, as discussed in paragraph 7 of SAS No. 69.

The AICPA Audit and Accounting Guide, which contains auditing guidance, is an interpretive publication pursuant to SAS No. 95, *Generally Accepted Auditing Standards*. Interpretive publications are recommendations on the application of SASs in specific circumstances, including engagements for entities in specialized industries. Interpretive publications are issued under the authority of the Auditing Standards Board. The members of the Auditing Standards Board have found this Guide to be consistent with existing SASs.

The auditor should be aware of and consider interpretive publications applicable to his or her audit. If the auditor does not apply the auditing guidance included in an applicable interpretive publication, the auditor should be prepared to explain how he or she complied with the SAS provisions addressed by such auditing guidance.

Public Accounting Firms Registered With the PCAOB

Subject to the Securities and Exchange Commission (Commission) oversight, Section 103 of the Sarbanes-Oxley Act (Act) authorizes the Public Company Accounting Oversight Board (PCAOB) to establish auditing and related attestation, quality control, ethics, and independence standards to be used by registered public accounting firms in the preparation and issuance of audit reports as required by the Act or the rules of the Commission. Accordingly, public accounting firms registered with the PCAOB are required to adhere to all PCAOB standards in the audits of issuers, as defined by the Act, and other entities when prescribed by the rules of the Commission. (See the Preface for further discussion.)

Mark M. Bielstein, *Chair*
Accounting Standards Executive
Committee

John A. Fogarty, *Chair*
Accounting Standards Board

Agribusiness Special Committee (1987)

The AICPA gratefully acknowledges Robert D. Beerup and Joseph Daughhetee for their assistance in review of the conforming changes for the May 2004 edition of this Guide.

AICPA Staff

Yelena Mishkevich
Technical Manager
Accounting and Auditing Publications

This edition of the Audit and Accounting Guide *Agricultural Producers and Agricultural Cooperatives*, has been modified by the AICPA staff to include certain changes necessary due to the issuance of authoritative pronouncements since the Guide was originally issued. This Guide reflects relevant guidance contained in authoritative pronouncements through May 1, 2004:

- FASB Statement No. 150, *Accounting for Certain Financial Instruments With Characteristics of Both Liabilities and Equity*, and Revised FASB Statements issued from May 1, 2003 through May 1, 2004, including

  FASB Statement No. 132 (revised 2003), *Employers' Disclosures About Pensions and Other Postretirement Benefits*

- FASB Interpretation No. 46 (revised December 2003), *Consolidation of Variable Interest Entities*

- FASB Technical Bulletin 01-1, *Effective Date for Certain Financial Institutions of Certain Provisions of Statement 140 Related to the Isolation of Transferred Financial Assets*

- FASB Staff Positions issued through May 1, 2004

- FASB Emerging Issues Task Force (EITF) consensus positions adopted at meetings of the EITF held through March 2004

- Practice Bulletin No. 15, *Accounting by the Issuer of Surplus Notes*

- SAS No. 101, *Auditing Fair Value Measurements and Disclosures*

- SOP 03-5, *Financial Highlights of Separate Accounts: An Amendment to the Audit and Accounting Guide* Audits of Investment Companies

- SSAE No. 12, *Amendment to Statement on Standards for Attestation Engagements No. 10*, Attestation Standards: Revision and Recodification

Users of this Guide should consider pronouncements issued subsequent to those listed above to determine their effect on entities covered by this Guide.

The changes made are identified in a schedule in appendix E of the Guide. The changes do *not* include all those that might be considered necessary if the Guide were subjected to a comprehensive review and revision.

This edition includes Statement of Position 85-3, *Accounting by Agricultural Producers and Agricultural Cooperatives*. In using this Guide, readers should refer to the material in the Statement of Position (appendix C).

Preface

This guide has been prepared to assist the independent auditor in auditing and reporting on financial statements of agricultural producers and agricultural cooperatives by describing relevant matters unique to the industry. It is intended—

- To provide background information on the nature and characteristics of the agricultural industry.
- To assist agricultural producers and cooperatives in applying generally accepted accounting principles.
- To assist the independent auditor in applying generally accepted auditing standards and knowledge of generally accepted accounting principles to determine whether generally accepted accounting principles have been applied by management, which has the primary responsibility for financial statements.

Generally accepted auditing standards and accounting principles are applicable to all types of agribusiness. The general application of these standards and principles is not discussed herein; rather, this guide focuses on the special problems inherent in auditing and reporting on the financial statements of agricultural producers and agricultural cooperatives.

This guide contains some suggested auditing procedures, but detailed internal control questionnaires and audit programs are not included. The nature, timing, and extent of auditing procedures are matters of professional judgment and will vary depending on the degree of audit risk and materiality.

This guide also includes information regarding statutory rules and regulations applicable to the industry and illustrations of the form and content of financial statements of agricultural producers and agricultural cooperatives and the independent auditor's reports thereon.

Statement of Position (SOP) 85-3, *Accounting by Agricultural Producers and Agricultural Cooperatives,* is included as an appendix to this document, and its recommendations on accounting for agricultural producers and cooperatives are an integral part of this guide. SOP 85-3 and the accounting provisions of this guide do *not* apply to personal financial statements of agricultural producers or statements prepared on a comprehensive basis of accounting other than generally accepted accounting principles (for example, the income tax or the cash basis of accounting). They also do not apply to growers of timber; growers of pineapple and sugarcane in tropical regions; raisers of animals for competitive sports; or merchants or noncooperative processors of agricultural products that purchase commodities from growers, contract harvesters, or others serving agricultural producers.

Effective Date

The provisions for this guide shall be effective for audits of financial statements for periods ending on or after December 31, 1987.

Agribusiness Special Committee

Substantial Changes to Audit Process Proposed

(Note: This discussion is not applicable to public accounting firms registered with the Public Company Accounting Oversight Board and their associated persons in connection with their audits of issuers as defined by the Sarbanes-Oxley Act, and other entities when prescribed by the rules of the Securities and Exchange Commission.)

In December 2002, the AICPA's Auditing Standards Board (ASB) issued an exposure draft proposing seven new Statements on Auditing Standards (SASs) relating to the auditor's risk assessment process. The ASB believes that the requirements and guidance provided in the proposed SASs, if adopted, would result in a substantial change in audit practice and in more effective audits. The primary objective of the proposed SASs is to enhance auditors' application of the audit risk model in practice by requiring:

- More in-depth understanding of the entity and its environment, including its internal control, to identify the risks of material misstatement in the financial statements and what the entity is doing to mitigate them.
- More rigorous assessment of the risks of material misstatement of the financial statements based on that understanding.
- Improved linkage between the assessed risks and the nature, timing and extent of audit procedures performed in response to those risks.

The exposure draft consists of the following proposed SASs:

- *Amendment to Statement on Auditing Standards No. 95,* Generally Accepted Auditing Standards
- *Audit Evidence*
- *Audit Risk and Materiality in Conducting an Audit*
- *Planning and Supervision*
- *Understanding the Entity and Its Environment and Assessing the Risks of Material Misstatement*
- *Performing Audit Procedures in Response to Assessed Risks and Evaluating the Audit Evidence Obtained*
- *Amendment to Statement on Auditing Standards No. 39,* Audit Sampling

The proposed SASs establish standards and provide guidance concerning the auditor's assessment of the risks of material misstatement in a financial statement audit, and the design and performance of audit procedures whose nature, timing, and extent are responsive to the assessed risks. Additionally, the proposed SASs establish standards and provide guidance on planning and supervision, the nature of audit evidence, and evaluating whether the audit evidence obtained affords a reasonable basis for an opinion regarding the financial statements under audit.

Readers can access the proposed standards at AICPA Online (www.aicpa.org) and should be alert to future progress on this project.

Applicability of Requirements of the Sarbanes-Oxley Act of 2002, Related Securities and Exchange Commission Regulations, and Standards of the Public Company Accounting Oversight Board

Publicly-held companies and other "issuers" (see definition below) are subject to the provisions of the Sarbanes-Oxley Act of 2002 (Act) and related Securities and Exchange Commission (SEC) regulations implementing the Act. Their outside auditors are also subject to the provisions of the Act and to the rules and standards issued by the Public Company Accounting Oversight Board (PCAOB).

Presented below is a summary of certain key areas addressed by the Act, the SEC, and the PCAOB that are particularly relevant to the preparation and issuance of an issuer's financial statements and the preparation and issuance of an audit report on those financial statements. However, the provisions of the Act, the regulations of the SEC, and the rules and standards of the PCAOB are numerous and are not all addressed in this section or in this Guide. Issuers and their auditors should understand the provisions of the Act, the SEC regulations implementing the Act, and the rules and standards of the PCAOB, as applicable to their circumstances.

Definition of an Issuer

The Act states that the term "issuer" means an issuer (as defined in section 3 of the Securities Exchange Act of 1934 (15 U.S.C. 78c)), the securities of which are registered under section 12 of that Act (15 U.S.C. 78l), or that is required to file reports under section 15(d) (15 U.S.C. 78o(d)), or that files or has filed a registration statement that has not yet become effective under the Securities Act of 1933 (15 U.S.C. 77a et seq.), and that it has not withdrawn.

Issuers, as defined by the Act, and other entities when prescribed by the rules of the SEC (collectively referred to in this Guide as "issuers" or "issuer") and their public accounting firms (who must be registered with the PCAOB) are subject to the provisions of the Act, implementing SEC regulations, and the rules and standards of the PCAOB, as appropriate.

Non-issuers are those entities not subject to the Act or the rules of the SEC.

Guidance for Issuers

Management Assessment of Internal Control

As directed by Section 404 of the Act, the SEC adopted final rules requiring companies subject to the reporting requirements of the Securities Exchange Act of 1934, other than registered investment companies and certain other entities (e.g., 11-K filers), to include in their annual reports a report of management on the company's internal control over financial reporting. See the SEC web site at www.sec.gov/rules/final/33-8238.htm for the full text of the regulation.

The SEC rules clarify that management's assessment and report is limited to *internal control over financial reporting*. The SEC's definition of internal control encompasses the Committee of Sponsoring Organizations of the Treadway Commission (COSO) definition but the SEC does not mandate that the entity use COSO as its criteria for judging effectiveness.

Under the SEC rules, the company's annual 10-K must include:

1. Management's Annual Report on Internal Control Over Financial Reporting
2. Attestation Report of the Registered Public Accounting Firm
3. Changes in Internal Control Over Financial Reporting

The SEC rules also require management to evaluate any change in the entity's internal control that occurred during a fiscal quarter and that has materially affected, or is reasonably likely to materially affect, the entity's internal control over financial reporting.

Audit Committees and Corporate Governance

Section 301 of the Act establishes requirements related to the makeup and the responsibilities of an issuer's audit committee. Among those requirements—

- Each member of the audit committee must be a member of the board of directors of the issuer, and otherwise be independent.

- The audit committee of an issuer is directly responsible for the appointment, compensation, and oversight of the work of any registered public accounting firm employed by that issuer.
- The audit committee shall establish procedures for the "receipt, retention, and treatment of complaints" received by the issuer regarding accounting, internal controls, and auditing.

In April 2003, the SEC adopted a rule to direct the national securities exchanges and national securities associations to prohibit the listing of any security of an issuer that is not in compliance with the audit committee requirements mandated by the Act.

Disclosure of Audit Committee Financial Expert and Code of Ethics

In January 2003, the SEC adopted amendments requiring issuers, other than registered investment companies, to include two new types of disclosures in their annual reports filed pursuant to the Securities Exchange Act of 1934. These amendments conform to Sections 406 and 407 of the Act and relate to disclosures concerning the audit committee's financial expert and code of ethics relating to the companies' officers. An amendment specifies that these disclosures are only required for annual reports.

Certification of Disclosure in an Issuer's Quarterly and Annual Reports

Section 302 of the Act requires the Chief Executive Officer (CEO) and Chief Financial Officer (CFO) of each issuer to prepare a statement to accompany the audit report to certify the "appropriateness of the financial statements and disclosures contained in the periodic report, and that those financial statements and disclosures fairly present, in all material respects, the operations and financial condition of the issuer."

In August 2002, the SEC adopted final rules for Certification of Disclosure in Companies' Quarterly and Annual Reports in response to Section 302 of the Act. CEOs and CFOs are now required to certify the financial and other information contained in quarterly and annual reports.

Improper Influence on Conduct of Audits

Section 303 of the Act makes it unlawful for any officer or director of an issuer to take any action to fraudulently influence, coerce, manipulate, or mislead any auditor engaged in the performance of an audit for the purpose of rendering the financial statements materially misleading. In April 2003, the SEC adopted rules implementing these provisions of the Act.

Disclosures in Periodic Reports

Section 401(a) of the Act requires that each financial report of an issuer that is required to be prepared in accordance with generally accepted accounting principles (GAAP) shall "reflect all material correcting adjustments . . . that have been identified by a registered accounting firm . . . " In addition, "each annual and quarterly financial report . . . shall disclose all material off-balance sheet transactions" and "other relationships" with "unconsolidated entities" that may have a material current or future effect on the financial condition of the issuer.

In January 2003, the SEC adopted rules that require disclosure of material off-balance sheet transactions, arrangements, obligations, and other relationships of the issuer with unconsolidated entities or other persons, that may have a material current or future effect on financial condition, changes in financial condition, results of operations, liquidity, capital expenditures, capital resources, or significant components of revenues or expenses. The rules require an issuer to provide an explanation of its off-balance sheet arrangements in a separately captioned subsection of the Management's Discussion and Analysis section of an issuer's disclosure documents.

Guidance for Auditors

The Act mandates a number of requirements concerning auditors of issuers, including mandatory registration with the PCAOB, the setting of auditing standards, inspections, investigations, disciplinary proceedings, prohibited activities, partner rotation, and reports to audit committees, among others. Auditors of issuers should familiarize themselves with applicable provisions of the Act and the standards of the PCAOB. The PCAOB continues to establish rules and standards implementing provisions of the Act concerning the auditors of issuers.

Applicability and Integration of Generally Accepted Auditing Standards and Public Company Accounting Oversight Board Standards

AICPA members who perform auditing and other related professional services have been required to comply with Statements on Auditing Standards (SASs) promulgated by the AICPA Auditing Standards Board (ASB). These standards constitute what is known as "generally accepted auditing standards" (GAAS). In the past, the ASB's auditing standards have applied to audits of *all* entities. However, as a result of the passage of the Act, auditing and related professional practice standards to be used in the performance of and reporting on audits of the financial statements of issuers are now established by the PCAOB.

Specifically, the Act authorizes the PCAOB to establish auditing and related attestation, quality control, ethics, and independence standards to be used by registered public accounting firms in the preparation and issuance of audit reports for entities subject to the Act or the rules of the SEC. Accordingly, public accounting firms registered with the PCAOB are required to adhere to all PCAOB standards in the audits of "issuers," as defined by the Act, and other entities when prescribed by the rules of the SEC.

For those entities not subject to the Act or the rules of the SEC, the preparation and issuance of audit reports remain governed by GAAS as issued by the ASB.

Extensive Guidance Available in AICPA *Professional Standards*

The AICPA *Professional Standards* and *Codification of Auditing Standards* contains a thorough section that provides important information and guidance about:

- The applicability and integration of GAAS and PCAOB standards;
- Standards applicable to the audits of non-issuers;
- Standards applicable to the audits of issuers;
- The PCAOB's adoption of interim standards;
- Standards applicable if a non-issuer's financial statements are audited in accordance with PCAOB standards; and,
- Applicability of GAAS to audits of issuers

GAAS and PCAOB Standards Included in This Guide

As the ASB and the PCAOB move forward in establishing auditing standards for entities within their respective jurisdictions, this Guide will present both

GAAS and PCAOB standards, as applicable depending on the auditing guidance

GAAS and PCAOB standards, as applicable depending on the auditing guidance presented in this Guide. Moreover, if differences between GAAS and PCAOB standards emerge, the auditing guidance in this Guide will integrate both sets of standards, as applicable, in order to offer practitioners a seamless source of auditing standards applicable to non-issuers and those applicable to issuers.

Major Existing Differences Between GAAS and PCAOB Standards

At the time of development of this Guide, the major differences between GAAS and final PCAOB standards approved by the SEC are as follows:

- Concurring Partner—PCAOB Rule 3400T requires the establishment of policies and procedures for a concurring review (generally the SECPS membership rule).[1]
- Communication of Firm Policy—PCAOB Rule 3400T requires registered firms to communicate through a written statement to all professional firm personnel the broad principles that influence the firm's quality control and operating policies and procedures on, at a minimum, matters that relate to the recommendation and approval of accounting principles, present and potential client relationships, and the types of services provided, and inform professional firm personnel periodically that compliance with those principles is mandatory (generally the SECPS membership rule).
- Affiliated Firms—PCAOB Rule 3400T requires registered firms that are part of an international association to seek adoption of policies and procedures by the international organization or individual foreign associated firms consistent with PCAOB standards.
- Partner Rotation—PCAOB Rule 3600T requires compliance with the SEC's independence rules which include partner rotation.
- Continuing Professional Education (CPE) Requirements—PCAOB Rule 3400T requires registered accounting firms to ensure that all of their professionals participate in at least 20 hours of qualifying CPE every year (generally the SECPS membership rule).
- Independence Matters—PCAOB Rule 3600T requires compliance with the SEC's independence rules and Standards No. 1, 2 and 3, and Interpretations 99-1, 00-1, and 00-2 of the Independence Standards Board.

Proposed PCAOB Auditing Standards and Proposed Changes to the PCAOB Interim Auditing Standards

As of the publication of this Guide, certain PCAOB standards and rules have been issued as final pronouncements, but are awaiting SEC approval. As such, these standards and rules are not yet effective. In addition, the PCAOB has issued exposure drafts of proposed standards and rules. Presented below is a table presenting certain key PCAOB proposed standards and rules that are particularly relevant to the audit of financial statements and how they may significantly affect the audits of issuers.

Auditors of issuers should be alert to the final resolution of these matters. If these standards are approved by the SEC, auditors of issuers will be required to comply with additional responsibilities and procedures. Furthermore, sections of the existing PCAOB interim auditing standards will be amended and superseded.

---

[1] Firms that were not members of the AICPA's SECPS as of April 16, 2003 do not have to comply with this requirement.

PCAOB Standard or Exposure Draft	Status	Explanation and Affect on Existing PCAOB Standards	PCAOB Website Link
Auditing Standard No. 2, *An Audit of Internal Control Over Financial Reporting Performed in Conjunction With an Audit of Financial Statements*	Issued as a final standard by the PCAOB; awaiting SEC approval	This standard establishes requirements and provides directions that apply when an auditor is engaged to audit both an issuer's financial statements and management's assessment of the effectiveness of internal control over financial reporting. This standard is the standard on attestation engagements referred to in Section 404(b) of the Act. Amendments to the PCAOB's interim standards as a result of the issuance of this standard are handled in the proposed auditing standard below.	www.pcaobus.org/rules/Release-20040308-1a.pdf
Proposed Auditing Standard, *Conforming Amendments to PCAOB Interim Standards Resulting From the Adoption of PCAOB Auditing Standard No. 2*	Issued as an exposure draft by the PCAOB	This standard proposes conforming amendments to the PCAOB interim auditing standards as a result of the issuance of PCAOB Auditing Standard No. 2. Sections of the PCAOB interim auditing standards that would be affected include: AU sec. 310, *Appointment of the Independent Auditor*; AU sec. 311, *Planning and Supervision*; AU sec. 312, *Audit Risk and Materiality in Conducting an Audit*; AU sec. 313, *Substantive Tests Prior to the Balance-Sheet Date*; AU sec. 316, *Consideration of Fraud in a Financial Statement Audit*; AU sec. 319, *Consideration of Internal Control in a Financial Statement Audit*; AU sec. 322, *The Auditor's Consideration of the Internal Audit Function in an Audit of Financial Statements*; AU sec. 324, *Service Organizations*; AU sec. 325, *Communication of Internal Control Related Matters Noted in an Audit*; AU sec. 326, *Evidential Matter*; AU sec. 329, *Analytical Procedures*; AU sec. 332, *Auditing Derivative Instruments, Hedging Activities, and Investments in Securities*; AU sec. 333, *Management Representations*; AU sec. 339, *Audit Documentation*; AU sec. 342, *Auditing Accounting Estimates*; AU sec. 508, *Reports on Audited Financial Statements*; AU sec. 530, *Dating of the Independent Auditor's Report*; AU sec. 543, *Part of Audit Performed by Other Independent Auditors*; AU sec. 560, *Subsequent Events*; AU sec. 561, *Subsequent Discovery of Facts*	www.pcaobus.org/rules/Release-20040308-2.pdf

(continued)

AAG-APC

PCAOB Standard or Exposure Draft	Status	Explanation and Affect on Existing PCAOB Standards	PCAOB Website Link
		Existing at the Date of the Auditor's Report; AU sec. 711, *Filings Under Federal Securities Statutes*; AU sec. 722, *Interim Financial Information*; AT sec. 501, *Reporting on an Entity's Internal Control Over Financial Reporting*; ET sec. 101, *Independence*	
Auditing Standard No. 1, *References in Auditors' Reports to the Standards of the Public Company Accounting Oversight Board*	Issued as a final standard by PCAOB; approved by the SEC, May 14, 2004	This standard requires registered public accounting firms to include in their reports on engagements performed pursuant to the PCAOB's auditing and related professional practice standards, a reference to the standards of the PCAOB (United States).	www.pcaobus.org/rules/Release2003-025.pdf
Proposed Auditing Standard, *Audit Documentation and Proposed Amendment to Interim Auditing Standards*	Issued as an exposure draft by the PCAOB	This standard establishes general requirements for documentation the auditor should prepare and retain in connection with any engagement conducted in accordance with auditing and related professional practice standards of the PCAOB. This standard does not supplant specific documentation requirements of other PCAOB auditing and related professional practice standards. This proposed standard would supersede AU sec. 339, *Audit Documentation*, and amend AU sec. 543, *Part of Audit Performed by Other Independent Auditors*, of the PCAOB interim auditing standards.	www.pcaobus.org/rules/Release2003-023.pdf

Auditor Reports to Audit Committees

Section 204 of the Act requires the accounting firm to report to the issuer's audit committee all "critical accounting policies and practices to be used . . . all alternative treatments of financial information within [GAAP] that have been discussed with management . . . ramifications of the use of such alternative disclosures and treatments, and the treatment preferred" by the firm.

Audit Documentation

Section 103 of the Act instructs the PCAOB to require registered public accounting firms to "prepare, and maintain for a period of not less than 7 years, audit work papers, and other information related to any audit report, in sufficient detail to support the conclusions reached in such report." The PCAOB has issued a proposed auditing standard (see the table above) that responds to this directive. Also, in January 2003, the SEC adopted rules to require accounting firms to retain for seven years certain records relevant to their audits and reviews of issuers' financial statements.

Other Requirements

The Act contains requirements in a number of other important areas, and the SEC has issued implementing regulations in certain of those areas as well. For example,

- The Act prohibits auditors from performing certain non-audit or non-attest services. The SEC adopted amendments to its existing requirements regarding auditor independence to enhance the independence of accountants that audit and review financial statements and prepare attestation reports filed with the SEC. This rule conforms the SEC's regulations to Section 208(a) of the Act and, importantly, addresses the performance of non-audit services.

- The Act requires the lead audit or coordinating partner and the reviewing partner to rotate off of the audit every 5 years. (See SEC Releases 33-8183 and 33-8183A for SEC implementing rules.)

- The Act directs the PCAOB to require a second partner review and approval of audit reports (concurring review).

- The Act states that an accounting firm will not be able to provide audit services to an issuer if one of that issuer's top officials (CEO, Controller, CFO, Chief Accounting Officer, etc.) was employed by the firm and worked on the issuer's audit during the previous year.

TABLE OF CONTENTS

Contents

Contents

Part III—continued

PART I — Agricultural Producers

Chapter 1

Introduction

1.01 Agriculture ranks among the largest industries in the United States and, until recent times, was the country's principal occupation and employer. Although the number of people involved in agricultural production is still large, that number has been steadily shrinking as a result of increased farm productivity, a growth in the size of individual farms and ranches, and the population shift toward urban centers. Despite the trend toward larger business units, however, entities engaged in agriculture still range from small noncorporate family groups to publicly held multinational corporations.

1.02 For purposes of this guide, the term *agricultural producers* includes farmers and ranchers who grow or raise agricultural or horticultural products for sale or for use in the production of other agricultural or horticultural products. In their transactions with agricultural cooperatives, they may be referred to as *members* or *patrons*.

1.03 Audits of agricultural producers should be designed and conducted in the same manner as audits of other enterprises, giving due consideration to the size and nature of the organization and internal control. The auditing procedures suggested herein are presented to provide guidance on matters that are unique or significant to the industry, but they may not apply to all situations and are not intended to replace or limit the use of judgment in determining the nature, timing, and extent of audit procedures to be applied in a particular audit.

1.04 Sample financial statements, whose form and content are currently acceptable, are illustrated in the appendixes.

Chapter 2

Background Information

2.01 Organizations ranging from small proprietorships to large public companies engage in a variety of farming and ranching activities, including the following:

- Growing wheat, milo, corn, and other grains
- Growing soybeans, vegetables, sugar beets, and sugarcane
- Growing citrus fruits, other fruits, grapes, berries, and nuts
- Growing cotton and other vegetable fibers
- Operating nurseries
- Breeding and feeding cattle, hogs, and sheep, including wool production
- Operating dairies
- Raising fish and shellfish
- Operating poultry and egg-production facilities
- Breeding horses
- Raising mink, chinchilla, and similar small animals

Agricultural producers may be involved in one or more activities, and their practices and products may vary because of differences in temperature, soil, rainfall, and regional economics.

2.02 Agricultural producers primarily market their products directly to existing commercial enterprises, consume them in a related activity, such as the feeding of raised hay and grains to livestock, or market them through agricultural cooperatives. Agricultural cooperatives may act as agents and account for the separate products of each producer, or they may commingle the patrons' products and either market them in the form in which the products were received or process them before sale. Producers also sell some products through governmental programs. Prices of most agricultural products are determined by economic forces, but some product prices are established by federal and state regulatory agencies. Agricultural producers may use forward sales contracts, commodity futures contracts, or options to reduce the risks associated with fluctuating commodity prices.

2.03 Agricultural producers conduct their operations in various manners. Some agricultural producers manage the entire productive activities of their farms and ranches. Others conduct agricultural operations as tenants under cash or crop-sharing rental agreements. Terms of crop-sharing agreements usually provide for a portion of the crop to be sold for the account of or delivered to the landowner. The extent of the landowner's participation in costs, profits, and management depends on the terms of each agreement.

2.04 The daily activities of farmers and ranchers who produce market crops may also create additions to fixed assets. Examples include the addition of raised animals to a breeding herd and the construction of buildings, fences, and various types of land improvements by using the producer's equipment and employees.

2.05 Federal and state income tax laws have significantly affected the operations and accounting practices of agricultural producers. Some accounting practices have been partially justified based on their acceptance for income tax purposes, but these practices may not be in accordance with generally accepted accounting principles. Economic decisions and productive activities of many agricultural producers have also been influenced by government subsidy and credit programs.

Chapter 3

Financial Reporting Information Systems, Internal Control, and Other Accounting Considerations

Financial Reporting Information Systems[*]

3.01 More attention has been given to financial reporting information systems and practices in the agricultural industry in recent years because of the increased size and complexity of operating units as well as the greater number of formally educated and trained agricultural producers and managers. Many large private entities and publicly held corporations engaging in agricultural production have sophisticated financial reporting information systems. However, many producers maintain elementary accounting records that are used for both tax and financial accounting. There are numerous sources of accounting forms and systems designed for agricultural producers. In addition, many producers use cash basis accounting. SAS No. 55, *Consideration of Internal Control in a Financial Statement Audit*, as amended by SAS No. 78, *Consideration of Internal Control in a Financial Statement Audit: An Amendment to SAS No. 55*, and by SAS No. 94, *The Effect of Information Technology on the Auditor's Consideration of Internal Control in a Financial Statement Audit*, provides guidance to auditors about the effect of information technology on internal control and on the auditor's understanding of internal control and assessment of control risk. Auditors whose clients chose to outsource their computer processing functions should refer to SAS No. 70, *Service Organizations*,[1] as amended by SAS No. 88, *Service Organizations and Reporting on Consistency*, for guidance on the factors that an independent auditor should consider when auditing the financial statements of an entity that uses a service organization to process certain transactions.

---

[*] In March 2004, the PCAOB issued Auditing Standard No. 2, *An Audit of Internal Control Over Financial Reporting Performed in Conjunction With an Audit of Financial Statements*. At the time of development of this edition of the Guide, this Standard was not approved by the SEC and was therefore not effective. If approved by the SEC, this Standard would apply to audits of the financial statements of issuers, as defined by the Sarbanes-Oxley Act, and other entities when prescribed by the rules of the SEC (collectively referred to as "issuers"). PCAOB Auditing Standard No. 2 establishes requirements that apply when an auditor is engaged to audit both an issuer's financial statements and management's assessment of the effectiveness of internal control over financial reporting. Due to the issuance of PCAOB Auditing Standard No. 2, a related proposed Standard (PCAOB Release No. 2004-002) would amend and supersede certain sections of the PCAOB Interim Standards. See the Preface of this Guide for more detailed information. Registered public accounting firms must comply with the Standards of the PCAOB in connection with the preparation or issuance of any audit report on the financial statements of an issuer and in their auditing and related attestation practices. Registered public accounting firms auditing the financial statements of issuers should keep alert to final SEC approval of this PCAOB Standard.

[1] For more information on SAS No. 70 readers should refer to the Audit Guide entitled *Service Organizations: Applying SAS No. 70, as Amended*, which includes illustrative control objectives as well as interpretations that address the responsibilities of service organizations and service auditors with respect to forward-looking information and the risk of projecting evaluations of controls to future periods. The Guide also clarifies that the use of a service auditor's report should be restricted to existing customers and is not meant for potential customers.

Internal Control[*]

3.02 As in other small businesses, internal control of many small agricultural operations are weak because they typically have small or part-time accounting staffs and little or no segregation of duties. However, involvement of the owner/manager in the operations frequently provides some control, particularly over access to assets and authorization of transactions.

3.03 Large agricultural operators are likely to have adequate controls over critical functions, such as sales, costs of production, inventories of products and supplies, purchases and disbursements, equipment use, and personnel utilization.

Cost Accounting and Cost Allocations

3.04 Accounting for the cost of agricultural products is similar to accounting for the cost of manufactured products. However, agricultural producers are faced with significant problems of cost identification and determination because the same personnel and equipment are often used in the production and sale of products, administration, and construction and production of assets. In addition, producers may raise diverse crops and animals, which further complicates the process of cost allocation.

3.05 Certain production costs, such as those for seed, planting, feed, and fertilizer, may be allocated directly to a particular product. Other production costs may be accumulated by department or function and allocated on systematic and rational bases to various products through cost or support centers. For example, costs may be accumulated for machinery and equipment used for more than one agricultural activity and allocated to the activities based on usage records. Departments providing goods or services for more than one product are often called *cost centers* or *support centers* and may be established for the purpose of accumulating indirect costs and direct costs for activities such as irrigation and pest and disease control.

3.06 Production overhead includes all production costs that are common to various products, support centers, and other cost objectives. These costs should be accumulated for each period and allocated to products based on direct labor hours, machinery and equipment use, or another basis that correlates with the use of resources.

3.07 If overhead and support center costs are estimated in advance and allocated on an interim basis, under- or overapplied costs may result. Under- or overapplied costs should be allocated to cost of goods sold, inventories, and growing crops.

3.08 Costs should be allocated when one raised product is used in the development of another. For example, grain or hay raised by the producer may be used to feed livestock. The costs of producing the grain or hay should be accumulated and allocated to the cost of producing the livestock.

3.09 The accounting system of the agricultural producer should be designed to match costs and expenses with related revenues. Costs of resources that are expected to provide future benefits should be deferred as assets on the balance sheet. Costs without expected future benefits should be charged to expense as incurred.

---

[*] See footnote * to the "Financial Reporting Information Systems" section in this chapter.

3.10 Questions frequently arise about the accounting treatment of costs incurred for replanting, costs attributable to prior crops, double-cropping costs, and costs of crops that take over one year to mature. These items, which do not apply to orchards, vineyards, and groves, are discussed below.

Partial Replanting

3.11 Partial replanting occurs for a variety of reasons, including damage from insects, crop disease, and drought. Costs of replanting may include land preparation, irrigation, seed, and labor. If those costs are considered normal costs and, when combined with other capitalized costs, do not exceed estimated net realizable value, they should be included as part of the growing or harvested crop's cost. If the costs are abnormal or excessive, they should be charged to operations. (See "Normal Costs Versus Abnormal or Excessive Costs," paragraphs 3.17 and 3.18.)

Complete Replanting

3.12 Complete replanting of a field may occur at some point during the crop year for various reasons, including economic considerations. Generally, the costs incurred with respect to the crop removed should be charged to expense, and the cost of the new planting should be capitalized as the cost of the new crop. However, some costs incurred for an earlier planting may benefit a replanted crop and be appropriately considered costs of the new crop. Examples of such items include deep plowing, estimated residual value of earlier fertilizing, and seedbed preparation.

Double-Cropping

3.13 A parcel of land may be used for more than one crop in the same growing season. For example, winter wheat might be planted in the fall and harvested in early summer of the following year. Immediately following the wheat harvest, soybeans may be planted and harvested that fall. As a result, certain costs may be allocated to more than one crop. For example, the same land preparation or fertilizer costs may benefit both crops and should be allocated to each crop, either on the basis of the relative values of the two crops or on another logical basis.

Extended-Period Crops and Methods

3.14 Some crop costs, such as soil preparation, are incurred prior to planting and should be deferred and allocated to the growing crop. Other cultural practices, such as clearing the residue of harvested crops, cannot be performed or completed until after harvest, which may be in a succeeding year; those costs should be estimated, accrued, and allocated to the harvested crop. Some crops require more than one year to mature, and the costs should be deferred until harvest.

3.15 It is not uncommon for assets to be constructed by using labor and materials from the farm or ranch rather than by employing an outside contractor. When this occurs, the costs of materials, labor, machinery and equipment, and related overhead applicable to such assets should be capitalized. Ordinarily, the costs of constructed assets includes only the direct construction costs and allocated overhead costs. The overhead rate used in capitalization should generally not be higher than the rate used for product costing. Other general and administrative expenses should not be capitalized. The amount of costs capitalized for internally constructed assets generally should not be more than the estimated external purchase price of such assets.

3.16 The interest costs related to construction or production of major assets should be capitalized in accordance with Financial Accounting Standards Board (FASB) Statement No. 34, *Capitalization of Interest Cost*.

Normal Costs Versus Abnormal or Excessive Costs

3.17 In order to record assets at amounts that do not defer losses to future periods, the producer should distinguish normal costs from abnormal costs. (Accounting Research Study No. 13, *The Accounting Basis of Inventories*, contains discussions of "abnormal costs" and "normalizing direct costs" that may be useful in distinguishing normal costs from abnormal costs.) Identification of abnormal costs involves consideration of the producer's performance, which can be measured by various statistics, such as utilization rates, per-acre crop yields, and insecticide application rates. Regional averages, the experience of others producing the same or similar products in a comparable area, and the opinions of specialists may be used to determine the level of performance that represents an acceptable standard of achievement under ordinary operating conditions.

3.18 Identification of abnormal costs of agricultural assets may require a general knowledge of the normal loss rate of animals, trees, or vines. No separate accounting is necessary for normal losses. When abnormal losses occur in a particular year, the undepreciated costs of lost animals, trees, or vines should be charged to current operations. In some cases the auditor may need to consider the use of specialists in determining normal loss rates (see Statement on Auditing Standards (SAS) No. 73, *Using the Work of a Specialist*).

Chapter 4

*Engagement Planning for Agricultural Producers**

4.01 SAS No. 22, *Planning and Supervision*, provides general guidance to the auditor for planning an audit engagement. To assist in planning the audit of an agricultural producer, numerous publications are available that contain detailed descriptions of most production operations. Such publications are available from U.S. government agencies, state agricultural universities, agricultural extension services, and commodity and trade organizations (See appendix D—*Information Sources*.)

4.02 Several unique planning considerations in the audit of an agricultural producer include—

1. The relationship of the producer's fiscal year-end to the harvest cycle of the producer's major crops. (For example, a producer with a fiscal year ending on June 30 whose major crop is rice will have a growing crop for the auditor to consider at year-end; however, the auditor for a similar producer with a fiscal year ending on December 31 would not have that same concern.)

2. The existence of share-crop arrangements. (For example, the auditor should consider terms of the share-crop agreement, title to the growing or harvested crops, possibility of inventory and accounting distortions because of planting schedules and different fiscal years, and the landowner's right to participate in management decisions, including the planting and sale of crops.)

3. Special conditions affecting the producer's crops, plants, and animals, such as diseases and unfavorable weather conditions. (For example, yields expected for a tree-fruit crop may be adversely affected to such a degree by weather conditions that accumulated costs may exceed inventory values. When these costs are increased by growing and harvest costs yet to be incurred, they may exceed anticipated crop revenues.)

4. Government regulations affecting the producer. (For example, the producer may be adversely affected by changes in the farm program or by local restrictions on the use of herbicides, pesticides, or fungicides.)

5. The need for the services of a specialist to evaluate the quality of the producer's crops, plants, or animals. (For example, in some instances the auditors may not possess the knowledge or experience to evaluate the health of plants and animals, estimate crop quality and expected yields, or recognize the existence of disease, infestations, etc.) (See SAS No. 73, *Using the Work of a Specialist*).

6. Availability of specialized information. Information regarding subsidy programs, historical crop yields, and general information regarding

---

* Auditors of issuers need to refer to the Preface of this Guide for important information related to the PCAOB.

local area conditions is available from the Department of Agriculture's Agricultural Stabilization and Conservation Service (ASCS), university extension services, and other sources.

Chapter 5

Inventories

Accounting for Inventories

5.01 Inventories of agricultural producers include growing crops, developing animals to be held for sale, harvested crops, livestock held for sale, and secondary products, such as calves from dairy herds and wool from sheep.

5.02 Growing crops and developing animals to be held for sale should be valued at the lower of cost or market. Inventories of harvested crops and livestock held for sale may be valued at the lower of cost or market or, in accordance with established industry practice, at sales price less estimated costs of disposal, when all the following conditions exist:

1. The product has a reliable, readily determinable, and realizable market price.

2. The product has relatively insignificant and predictable costs of disposal.

3. The product is available for immediate delivery.

5.03 For the purpose of this section, market means net realizable value as defined in statement 6 of chapter 4 in Accounting Research Bulletin No. 43 and discussed later in this section of the guide. A reliable market price should be found in an established market for products that are comparable to the product being valued and that do not vary significantly because of differences in grade or variety.

5.04 The product should be located sufficiently close to the marketplace to make delivery practical without significant costs or time delays. These circumstances affect the amount and predictability of market prices. In addition, the marketing procedures should be well established so that transportation and other disposal costs, which should be relatively small, can be estimated with reasonable accuracy.

Net Realizable Value

5.05 Inventories of harvested crops and livestock held for sale and commonly referred to as valued at market are actually valued at net realizable value. Thus, whether harvested crops and livestock held for sale are valued at market or at the lower of cost or market, it is necessary to determine the net realizable value of those inventories. At times, net-realizable-value calculations are required for growing crops and developing animals. For these categories, costs to complete, including direct costs, production overhead, and costs of disposal should be estimated and deducted from the anticipated sales prices to determine the net realizable value for the growing crops and developing animals and to compare it to costs incurred.

5.06 Determining net realizable value requires estimating selling prices and related costs of disposal in the ordinary course of business. The entity's involvement with derivative instruments and hedging activities may also need to be considered. Disposal costs include handling, packing, transportation costs identified with sale of the specific product, and selling expenses such as commissions and other types of direct sales expense.

5.07 Sources of market information for agricultural commodities are numerous. They include quoted daily prices for traded commodities such as grains and livestock. For other commodities, information may be available from local dealers, crop-reporting services, commercial lending institutions, county extension services, and trade publications. The reputation and credibility of the information source should be considered. The market data should be adjusted to the local price because there are usually significant variations between the local and central market prices, reflecting, at the least, the freight differential. In addition, prices of most agricultural products will depend on their grade classifications, which should be considered in determining net realizable value.

5.08 Any estimate of net realizable value by the producer should be based on the most reliable evidence available at the balance sheet date. If a material variation from that amount exists prior to the date the financial statements are issued, the auditor should refer to SAS No. 1, section 560, *Subsequent Events,* for guidance regarding consideration of subsequent events.

An Overview of the Audit of Inventories

5.09 Audit objectives include (*a*) obtaining reasonable assurance that inventory quantities represent all agricultural products and animals belonging to the producer and (*b*) determining that an acceptable valuation method has been properly and consistently applied.[1] If a cost method is used to value inventories, cost should not exceed net realizable value. Adequate disclosure related to inventories should be made.

5.10 Audit procedures for inventories generally are similar to those performed in the audit of manufacturing entities. Unique audit risks may require modification of those procedures, as described here.

1. When no documents exist to evidence title to raised products, reviews of cost records, yield statistics, and supporting documents should indicate the nature and extent of the farming activity and thus provide that evidence.

2. When there is a lack of documentary evidence to support the ownership of raised livestock, the number of animals represented as produced for a period may be tested for reasonableness by applying normal productivity rates to the productive animals in the breeding herd. Inspection of records evidencing real estate ownership may provide additional support for ownership of crops and livestock on the land. Tenant lease agreements should also be considered.

3. Inventories of agricultural products are often stored in public warehouses. The auditor should perform those procedures considered necessary (*a*) to obtain reasonable assurance that the inventories exist, are owned by the entity, and are in a marketable condition and (*b*) to determine whether they are pledged as collateral for loans. (See SAS No. 1, section 331.14, *Inventories,* as amended by SAS No. 43, *Omnibus Statement on Auditing Standards.*)

---

[1] The level of the auditor's responsibility for performing procedures or achieving objectives can be described in two ways—with the terms *assurance* or *risk*. Assurance is the complement or converse of risk. SAS No. 47, *Audit Risk and Materiality in Conducting an Audit,* discusses reducing audit risk to an appropriately low level. The term *reasonable assurance* is used in this guide to describe the same level of the auditor's responsibility.

Chapter 6

*Specific Accounting Principles and Auditing Considerations**

Field and Row Crops

Background and Unique Characteristics

6.01 Field and row crops with cycles of less than one year are generally classed as annuals. These crops include wheat, barley, milo, corn, soybeans, sugar beets, tobacco, cotton, crops raised for seed, tomatoes, lettuce, beans, cabbages, and melons.

6.02 Field and row crops are usually planted from seeds or are transplanted from beds and develop to the point of harvest within several months. In certain areas, when weather conditions permit, two and sometimes three different crops can be raised and harvested sequentially from the same field during one year. These practices are referred to as *double-* and *triple-cropping*.

6.03 Good management of field and row crops demands careful protection from spoilage. The delicate nature of some crops requires quick handling from harvest to storage because the product may become worthless in a short period of time. Current methods of harvesting and handling usually prevent spoilage from becoming a significant problem.

6.04 In recent years hybridization has resulted in plant varieties that carry substantially improved growth, maturation, and yield characteristics compared with older varieties. The development of improved varieties has occurred simultaneously with improvements in both cultural techniques and harvesting equipment. These innovations have increased yields per acre, reduced per-unit costs, and enhanced the general economic value of those plantings.

Accounting Principles

6.05 Costs of growing crops should be accumulated until the time of harvest, subject to lower of cost or market adjustments. Harvested crops held for sale should be reported at the lower of cost or market or in accordance with established industry practice at market if certain conditions described in paragraph 39 of Statement of Position (SOP) 85-3, *Accounting by Agricultural Producers and Agricultural Cooperatives*, exist. (See appendix C for SOP 85-3.)

6.06 Cost centers may be established by field, crop, ranch, or other geographic area. To adequately allocate costs to inventories, each cost center should be charged with direct material and labor and an allocation of indirect costs. Where there are multiple crops, records should be maintained to provide a basis for allocation of total costs to the separate crops.

6.07 Most costs related to producing field and row crops benefit only the current-year crop (for example, furrows and beds constructed for annual plantings). However, certain costs may be expended for resources benefiting more than one crop year and should be allocated to the appropriate years. For instance,

---

* Auditors of issuers need to refer to the Preface of this Guide for important information related to the PCAOB.

in the production of rice crops the engineering and grading costs for *borders* (ridges used to retain water) may benefit several years. Such costs are properly included in property and equipment and amortized over their useful lives.

6.08 Generally, farming procedures undertaken after the current year harvest benefit the crop of the succeeding year. There may be instances, however, where additional costs such as costs of special tillage, chopping, or burning are required after harvest of a particular crop to overcome a physical or noxious condition. Those costs should be estimated and accrued as costs of the harvested crop.

6.09 In some agricultural operations a field or row crop is raised for use in the development of another product, such as grain or hay used by the producer to feed livestock. The costs involved in the production of the field or row crops for the producer's own use should be identified as part of the maintenance costs of the livestock and accounted for in the same manner as other maintenance costs, as described in "Accounting Principles for Breeding Animals," paragraphs 6.47 through 6.53, to follow.

Auditing Considerations

6.10 When planning the engagement, the auditor should inquire about the farming procedures and become familiar with the overall operation and any unusual events and practices.

6.11 The auditor should consider performing the following audit procedures for harvested and growing field and row crops:

1. Physically observing and reviewing crop maturity and quality

2. Confirming the existence of harvested crops stored in outside warehouses (see SAS No. 1, section 331.14, *Inventories*, as amended by SAS No. 43, *Omnibus Statement on Auditing Standards*)

3. Reviewing and testing the capitalized costs of growing and harvested crops for reasonableness

4. Determining that capitalized costs of crops do not exceed market

6.12 When records of ownership are inadequate or nonexistent, determining the ownership of harvested crops can present special audit risks. In those situations, evidence of crop ownership may be provided by a review of direct crop costs, harvesting and handling expenses, and applicable leases and tenant agreements.

6.13 Unique audit risks also may be encountered in reviewing the quality of harvested crops. When inventories include harvested crops, the auditor should seek reasonable assurance that the stored commodity is of acceptable variety and quality. Assessing the value of a commodity can be a demanding procedure. In addition to market conditions, the value will be influenced by physical condition, variety, and quality.

6.14 The physical state of the product may be affected by obvious conditions, such as mold, decay, or other evidence of physical spoilage, or by deterioration discernible only to those experienced and technically qualified. For instance, seed held in storage for long periods may suffer loss of germination potential that can only be detected by laboratory tests. Other damage may include insect infestations that require microscopic examination to determine the type and extent of deterioration.

6.15 The variety of a stored commodity may have a material influence on value. For instance, recent technical advances in hybridization have resulted in the development of varieties and strains of agricultural products far superior to the varieties they replaced. As a consequence, stored seeds of an old variety may have only a fraction of their former value. There have even been instances where inventories of plants and trees growing in nursery farms were obsolete before they were ready for market.

6.16 Quality, though similar to condition, is distinguishable from it. For instance, two groups of seeds may be in good condition and of the same variety but may have distinctive quality differences. One group may pass germination tests with high percentages, whereas the second group may have low percentages or undesirable germination qualities.

6.17 In reviewing the quantity, condition, quality, and relative value of agricultural products, the auditor should consider using specialists whose credentials demonstrate their ability to evaluate farm products. (See SAS No. 73.)

6.18 Special attention should be given to inventories of crops grown for seed. Although the commodity may be corn or some other grain, seed crops are significantly different from crops of the same product sold in the general market. Consequently, the auditor should refer to markets applicable to seed crops because general market prices may not be appropriate.

Orchards and Vineyards

Background and Unique Characteristics

6.19 Orchards and groves produce such commodities as citrus, walnuts, almonds, pecans, peaches, pears, apples, apricots, cherries, and avocados. There are many varieties and subvarieties of each. The term *vines*, for purposes of this section, refers primarily to grape vines, of which there are several hundred varieties.

6.20 Each variety and type of tree or vine requires a period of development to reach a stage of maturity at which it produces in commercial quantities. During this development period there are substantial expenditures for labor and material to shape and train the tree or vine into an efficient form. For instance, the lower limbs of fruit or nut trees are held apart to spread the tree and develop a wider and more open crown to improve productivity. In addition, trees are pruned and shaped in the early growth stages to encourage a lower profile. Such practices can limit the height of the tree and alter its shape to accommodate mechanical picking or more rapid picking from vehicles.

6.21 During the development period, trees and vines require grafting, pruning, spraying, cultivation, and similar care. Occasionally, row crops are grown between the rows of developing trees or vines to provide a supplemental source of revenue until the trees or vines reach maturity.

6.22 Although fruits, nuts, and grapes can be grown in most parts of the nation, different varieties may produce more effectively in particular geographic areas. As a result, the crop development periods and cultural cycles vary significantly in different geographic areas.

6.23 Trees and vines require several years of development before production occurs in commercial quantities. The costs of labor and materials to shape and train trees and vines constitute a significant portion of the costs incurred during the development years. During the last two or three years of the development period, it is not unusual for trees and vines to produce fruit or nuts in less than commercial quantities. Once the trees and vines have matured adequately, production generally continues for a number of years, depending upon the plant, soil, climate, and other influences. The productive lives of trees and vines with the same general classification may vary, depending on the particular variety.

6.24 The products of trees and vines require careful handling after harvest. They must be skillfully graded due to wide variations in quality. Then, because of the perishable nature of the products they can be downgraded or become worthless if not stored so that they are protected against temperature variations and insects.

Accounting Principles

6.25 Trees and vines may be planted and brought to production by the producer or on a contract basis. The young trees and vines are usually purchased as nursery stock and transplanted into the orchard or vineyard in the desired pattern. Cultural costs during the development period, including stakes and wires, grafting, and labor for pruning and forming, should be capitalized. Net proceeds from sales of products before commercial production begins should be applied to the capitalized cost of the plants, trees, or vines.

6.26 The productive lives of the trees or vines can usually be estimated by considering such factors as the geographical area (influence of water, humidity, and temperature), variety or classification of the plant, type of rootstock used, grafting and pruning practices, plant-spacing intervals, and picking or harvesting methods. The best sources of data regarding these factors are grower and commodity associations and the local agricultural extension service.

6.27 Not all plants in a developing orchard, vineyard, or grove will survive to a productive stage. Normal losses do not generally require an adjustment to reduce the capitalized cost of an orchard or grove. However, the capitalized cost of trees or vines lost through abnormal events, such as unusual disease, frost, or flood, should be written off in the year of the loss and the costs to replant should be capitalized. (The distinction between normal and abnormal is determined on the basis of the procedures discussed in "Normal Costs Versus Abnormal or Excessive Costs" in paragraphs 3.17 and 3.18 of this guide.)

6.28 Each orchard, vineyard, or grove may be considered a cost center, and all costs incurred prior to the time of commercial production should be accumulated in the property accounts. When production in commercial quantities begins, the accumulated costs should be depreciated over the estimated useful life of the particular orchard, vineyard, or grove.

6.29 Operators of orchards and vineyards should account for costs of growing and harvested crops in the same manner as other agricultural producers, as discussed in "Field and Row Crops," paragraphs 6.01 through 6.18 of this chapter. Growing costs include annual maintenance cost of the orchard or vineyard, such as cultivation, spraying, fertilizing and pruning; annual depreciation of the orchard or vineyard; and normal tree and vine replacement.

Auditing Considerations

6.30 Audit procedures for orchards and vineyards are similar to those performed for other types of property, plant, and equipment and may include—

1. Considering the relative health and conditions of the trees or vines.

2. Reviewing the estimated remaining productive lives of the trees or vines. This may require an annual inspection of the orchard or vineyard, and, when questions arise, the auditor may need to consult a specialist.

3. Testing total capitalized costs of orchards and vineyards to determine whether such costs are recoverable. In performing such tests, comparisons should be made with prevailing costs for similar orchards and vineyards and with data obtainable from state agricultural universities, agricultural extension services, and commodity and trade organizations.

6.31 In testing the recoverability of accumulated costs of growing crops, the auditor should consider prospective yield, weather conditions, expected market price, and ability to economically harvest and transport the crop to the marketplace. It is not uncommon for the net realizable value of a growing crop to be less than the accumulated costs. The auditor may perform the following audit procedures:

1. Testing the accumulation of costs of growing crops for accuracy of classification.

2. Comparing accumulated costs with market prices and estimated disposition costs.

3. Considering the physical condition of the inventory in reviewing its net realizable value. The use of a specialist may be advisable. (See SAS No. 73.)

Intermediate-Life Plants

Background and Unique Characteristics

6.32 Intermediate-life plants include perennial plants and vines that have growth cycles of more than one year. Such plants include artichokes, asparagus, various types of bush berries, kiwifruit, alfalfa, and grazing grasses. Those plants produce for more than one year, depending on the type of plant and the geographic area, but not as long as trees and vines.

Accounting Principles

6.33 Accounting principles for intermediate-life plants are similar to the principles applicable to orchards and vineyards.

6.34 Intermediate-life plants may be developed by the agricultural producer or developed by others on a contract basis. Costs of intermediate-life plants developed by the producer include costs of land preparation, plants, preparation of planting beds, stakes and wires, cultural care during the development period, and overhead. Accumulated costs for these plants and vines, whether acquired on a contract basis or self-developed, should be capitalized.

6.35 When production in commercial quantities begins, the capitalized costs should be depreciated over the estimated productive life of the plantings. Regional differences, climate and soil conditions, and cultural practices may affect the productive capacity and life of intermediate-life plants and should be considered when establishing depreciable lives. The capitalized costs should be classified with property, plant, and equipment; financial statement disclosure of the costs and estimated useful lives should be made.

6.36 After the development period, annual maintenance costs become a portion of the cost of the current-year crop, along with harvesting costs, depreciation of the plants, and allocated overhead costs. Annual maintenance costs include cultivation, spraying, pruning, and fertilizing. The harvested crop held for sale should be reported at the lower of cost or market or in accordance with established industry practice at market if certain conditions described in paragraph 39 of SOP 85-3, *Accounting by Agricultural Producers and Agricultural Cooperatives*, exist.

Auditing Considerations

6.37 Audit procedures for intermediate-life plants are similar to those performed for other types of property, plant, and equipment, and may include—

1. Physically observing the condition of the plants.

2. Testing accumulated costs for properly capitalized amounts.

3. Comparing accumulated costs to prevailing costs for similar plants.

4. Testing accumulated costs for recoverability. If there is a question about future productive capability of the plants, it may be necessary to consult a specialist. (For example, unusually heavy rainfall or inadequate drainage may have "drowned" all or a substantial portion of an alfalfa planting [an intermediate-life plant]; in this case, the auditor should consider whether the remaining deferred costs of that crop are recoverable and may need to consult a specialist.)

5. Testing the useful lives or depreciation rates used in accounting for the plants. Actual or anticipated production declines may lead to a revision of useful lives or depreciation rates.

Breeding and Production Animals

Background and Unique Characteristics

6.38 Breeding herds consist of mature and immature male and female animals, either of registered or commercial grade, that are maintained for their progeny. Registered herds are used to preserve or improve the desirable characteristics of the animals, and commercial herds provide animals for consumption. Registered animals are bred and retained on the basis of the demand for particular characteristics and their ability to reproduce animals with the same desirable attributes. The values of registered animals may be comparatively higher and significantly greater than those of commercial-grade animals.

6.39 Production animals provide a service or primary product other than their progeny. Examples are dairy cows (milk), poultry (meat and eggs), and sheep (meat and wool).

6.40 In many areas of the country, commercial-grade cattle are maintained on large grazing areas or on open ranges, such as land rented from the Bureau of Land Management, the U.S. Forest Service, or various state agencies. Range conditions and infrequent observation may result in a higher percentage of unbred females and lower calf-survival rates than those for animals confined in smaller areas and more closely observed.

6.41 Horses are still used by agricultural producers, particularly by those who raise cattle and sheep. Some have extensive programs for breeding, raising, and training the saddle horses used in their operations.

6.42 Dairy herds are used primarily for the production of milk that is often unprocessed when sold to a cooperative or other buyer. Calves are a secondary product of dairy operations and may be retained as replacement animals. Animals not selected as herd replacements, along with those later culled from the productive dairy herd, are usually sold for slaughter.

6.43 The marketing of milk is controlled in most states. In some jurisdictions the producer owns rights called *milk quotas* or *can contracts* that entitle the producer to sell the processor a stated quantity of milk per period. Those rights are separate from the milk-producing herd in some states, and in others they remain with the herd. If the rights are separate, they have a market value and may be purchased and sold.

6.44 Poultry operations may include the raising of birds for meat, the production of eggs for human consumption, and the raising of breeder pullets. Chicken and turkey operations are similar. There are usually three separate phases of poultry operations: brooder, meat, and eggs. All phases might be found in one integrated operation, or an operation might be limited to one phase. Examples are turkey operations that raise meat birds or chicken operations that raise broilers as the principal source of revenue. In either operation, hatchlings may be purchased from other producers.

6.45 Other examples of single-phase operations are brooder-chicken farms that produce layer pullets (young hens) and egg-laying units where the sale of eggs is the principal source of income. Income from the sale of older or "spent" hens for meat is nominal and incidental to an egg-laying operation.

6.46 Poultry operations can utilize the following: complex and costly brooder facilities; large flocks of breeder chickens and laying hens; extensive specialized buildings; feed mills and storage facilities; rooms for washing, candling, and packaging eggs; cold storage; transportation equipment; and manure-handling and manure-processing equipment. Around-the-clock intensive care of the flocks requires employees to be on duty or nearby at all times. Therefore, it is common for employee housing to be a significant part of the overall operating facilities.

Accounting Principles for Breeding Animals

6.47 Whether breeding animals are of registered or commercial grade, their purpose is to produce young animals. Thus, accounting for livestock operations usually requires accumulation of the annual maintenance costs of the breeding herd as a means of establishing the cost of young animals. Included in the total to be allocated to the animals produced are costs of feed, veterinary care, medicines, labor, land and pasture rent, and depreciation of the herd and facilities. Costs of maintaining raised animals prior to maturity or disposition are capitalized as an additional cost of the animals. Costs of raising the young animals should be accumulated and allocated on a rational basis. Not all young animals survive to maturity or disposition; normal losses of young animals are usually not expensed directly because total annual maintenance costs are assigned to the survivors. The accumulated costs of animals lost through causes considered abnormal should be written off in the period in which the abnormal losses occur. (See "Normal Costs Versus Abnormal or Excessive Costs" in paragraphs 3.17 and 3.18.)

6.48 Regardless of the size or quality of the herd, the accounting principles applicable to accumulating costs remain the same. The accounting system should provide accumulated costs of replacement animals as well as costs of animals culled.

6.49 When males are maintained for the breeding herd, the ownership and maintenance costs usually constitute a separate cost center. When artificial insemination is used, the costs of the semen and insemination process are direct costs. Practices of the producer will usually dictate the accounting methods to be used.

6.50 As the animals mature and costs are accumulated, the accounting considerations may vary depending on the future use of each animal. The usual alternatives include the following:

- Transfer to the breeding herd, in which case the costs would be accumulated until the animal is mature and the breeding process is begun. The costs then become part of the depreciable cost of the breeding herd.

- Sale of young animals to another breeder or feeder, in which case the costs would be accumulated until the animal is sold. A gain or loss equal to the sale proceeds, less the accumulated costs and the expenses of sale, would then be recognized.

- Retention until fattened and sold, in which case the costs of production, care, and feeding to date of sale are accumulated and charged to cost of sales.

6.51 Some producers raise feed for their animals. Costs of producing the feed should be considered a cost of the animals and capitalized or accounted for as a production cost based on classification of the animals.

6.52 The total capitalized costs of raised breeding animals, including interest required to be treated as a cost under FASB Statement No. 34 should generally not exceed the estimated external purchase price of such animals.

6.53 Generally, breeding animals are fixed assets and their costs should be depreciated over their useful lives. Immature animals are not considered to be in service until they reach maturity, at which time their accumulated costs become subject to depreciation. The same general accounting principles apply to all livestock, which includes cattle, hogs, sheep, and goats. Animals with short productive lives, such as poultry, may be classified as inventory.

Auditing Considerations for Breeding Animals

6.54 Major audit objectives for breeding animals include establishing the existence and proper valuation of the animals. The auditor may choose to perform audit procedures such as—

1. Physically observing the animals.

2. Reviewing and testing the applicable acquisition and accounting records.

3. Reviewing the reasonableness of the useful lives of the animals, the depreciation rates, and salvage values. The reasonableness of useful lives should be reviewed in light of the experience of similar operations in the same geographical area.

4. Observing and performing counts of animals. Special audit risks exist where animals are left on grazing areas or open ranges. In those situations, the auditor may need to perform or observe counts at interim periods or may decide to use the services of a specialist. (See SAS No. 73.) Test counts should be used only in those circumstances where controls and periodic independent observations have conclusively proven the integrity of the accounting system and related controls.

5. Considering the use of a specialist where it is necessary (a) to identify breeds; (b) to read brands, tattoos, ear tags, earmarks, and other special identification marks; or (c) to evaluate the quality of the animals.

Additional procedures are described in the section of this guide dealing with auditing considerations applicable to animals held for sale. (See "Auditing Considerations," paragraphs 6.69 and 6.70.)

Accounting Principles for Production Animals

6.55 Production animals generally are fixed assets subject to depreciation procedures described for breeding animals. The principles are similar to group depreciation methods applicable to other fixed assets.

6.56 When milk-marketing rights remain with the producing herd, it may be necessary to allocate acquisition costs between the animals and the rights. The costs allocated to the animals should be depreciated over their estimated useful lives. Costs allocated to the marketing rights should be accounted for in accordance with FASB Statement No. 142, *Goodwill and Other Intangible Assets.*[*]

6.57 The accounting principles for poultry operations are much the same as those for livestock, although the operating cycles are much shorter. The production costs of chickens raised for an egg-laying unit should include the initial cost of the birds (or, if hatched, the costs of eggs and hatching expenses), the costs of materials and labor, and allocated indirect costs during the prematurity period. These costs, less estimated salvage value of the chickens, should be amortized over the egg-laying period. Due to the short productive life of poultry, the cost of flocks may be classified as inventory.

6.58 Costs attributed to eggs produced for human consumption consist of the costs for maintaining the production flock, applicable overhead, and depreciation of the production flock and the facilities.

6.59 Some production animals produce more than one product. For example, sheep produce lambs, wool, and meat; dairy cattle produce milk, calves, and meat. The primary products are lambs and milk, whereas the secondary products are usually wool and calves. Costs may be allocated as either joint products or by-products depending on the estimated relative values of each. In most instances the meat, or slaughter value, of the production animal is considered salvage. The method of accounting should be determined by the amounts anticipated to be received for each product. Those amounts are affected by the breeding, production, and marketing practices of the producer.

Auditing Considerations for Production Animals

6.60 Audit procedures for production animals with extended productive lives are similar to those for breeding animals and other fixed assets. They include—

---

[*] A toolkit, *Auditing Fair Value Measurements and Disclosures: Allocations of the Purchase Price Under FASB Statement of Financial Accounting Standards No. 141*, Business Combinations, *and Tests of Impairment Under FASB Statements No. 142*, Goodwill and Other Intangible Assets, *and No. 144*, Accounting for the Impairment or Disposal of Long-Lived Assets, contains nonauthoritative guidance to help auditors understand and apply Statements on Auditing Standards when auditing fair value measurements and disclosures related to business combinations, goodwill and other intangible assets, and certain impairment situations. The guidance is illustrated in the context of a business combination since many of the key concepts and principles are revealed in this common business situation. However, the concepts and procedures described may also be useful when auditing goodwill and other intangible assets accounted for under FASB Statement No. 142 and when auditing impairment or disposal of assets accounted for under FASB Statement No. 144. Therefore, the illustrative audit program and illustrative disclosure checklist cover FASB Statements No. 142 and No. 144 in addition to FASB Statement No. 141. Additionally, the toolkit provides an overview of FASB Statements No. 142 and No. 144 and discusses certain auditing considerations. The toolkit is free and may be downloaded from www.aicpa.org/members/div/auditstd/fasb123002.asp.

1. Testing capitalized costs.

2. Reviewing the reasonableness of depreciation policies, including lives, depreciation rates, and salvage values.

3. Testing depreciation calculations.

4. Applying other procedures described in the sections of this guide dealing with auditing considerations applicable to breeding animals and animals held for sale [paragraphs 6.54, 6.69, and 6.70].

Animals Held for Sale

Background and Unique Characteristics

6.61 Animals held for sale include all the progeny of the breeding herds except those retained for the expansion or replacement of existing herds. In some operations, young animals are purchased and maintained until they develop further and are sold. Animals held for sale are usually not retained beyond the time they reach optimal size or weight because their value usually does not increase thereafter and may even decrease.

6.62 In this section, cattle operations are described in more detail than other animal-feeding operations because they have the longest operating cycle; however, the same principles apply to operations with shorter operating cycles. A calf will usually be kept with its mother from birth until the time it is weaned. These young animals, referred to as *weaners*, will then be placed on pasture for a period of months or sent to a feedlot.

6.63 Young feeder animals bought by producers in the spring of the year are often kept on large grazing areas or open ranges, where they are subject to the same physical conditions described for breeding herds, until the fall, when they are transferred to feedlots. Cattle feeders may transfer raised cattle to feedlots or purchase young cattle to be placed in feedlots.

6.64 Some feed producers and breeders supply young animals and chicks to other producers who raise the animals to maturity, and they provide breeding animals and dairy cows on a rental basis. Terms of the agreements under which these arrangements are made generally provide for sharing the income from the use and sale of the animals. These arrangements provide a source of capital for the producers and reduce their risk of loss; consequently, they are used extensively in cattle, hog, poultry, and dairy operations.

6.65 Agricultural producers also engage in farming for oysters, abalone, and catfish. The major differences between these operations and the ones already described usually relate to the length of the operating cycles, ease of identification of the operating cycles, ease of identification of the productive group (breeding versus held for sale) for costing purposes, the nature of certain costs, and the environment in which they live.

Accounting Principles

6.66 Animals held for sale are inventories of the producer and should be accounted for at the lower of cost or market, or under certain circumstances at sales price less estimated cost of disposal as explained in paragraph 62 of SOP 85-3 [Appendix C].

6.67 The costs of raised or purchased animals kept in grazing areas or open ranges are determined in the manner discussed in the section of this guide dealing with breeding animals [paragraphs 6.38 through 6.60].

6.68 Costs during the period the cattle are held in feeding pens should be readily determinable. The cattle are in a controlled environment for a relatively short period of time, usually not over six months, and are typically segregated into pens by expected date of slaughter. Accordingly, costs can frequently be aggregated by pens. The purchase price (or transferred cost, if applicable), labor and yard expenses (including depreciation of equipment and pens), veterinary supplies, and feed represent the total costs of the animals at the time of slaughter.

Auditing Considerations

6.69 The audit procedures applied in animal-feeding operations should be designed to deal with the special audit risks resulting from the lack of documents to evidence the ownership of raised animals. Evidence of ownership of raised animals may be obtained by performing tests that apply the usual productivity rates to the number of breeding animals. However, possession of the animals does not necessarily establish ownership. In some cases, the presence of animals without proof of ownership or purchase records may indicate the existence of a leasing or profit-sharing arrangement. Records of feed consumption may provide an indication of the total number of animals in the possession of the producer. Moreover, the management representation letter[1] should contain an affirmation of ownership for the recorded number of animals.

6.70 In addition, the auditor should review the adequacy of the accounting system and related controls, and consider performing the following audit procedures:

1. Observing test counts or total counts of animals held for sale, depending on the adequacy of controls.

2. Testing the costs capitalized for the animals.

3. Obtaining reliable estimates of the weight and quantity of the animals for valuation purposes.

4. Testing the net realizable value of the animals by reference to quoted market prices. Consideration should be given to local market prices that may differ from regional prices.

Land Development Costs

Background and Unique Characteristics

6.71 The following discussion of land development costs is limited to development costs applicable to the creation of productive assets possessing identifiable value and expected to create future income. These costs generally include costs of changes to make land suitable for general agricultural use, but they may also include improvements to land already used for agricultural production. Examples of land development activities are clearing brush, removing rocks, and leveling.

---

[1] SAS No. 85, *Management Representations*, as amended by SAS No. 89, *Audit Adjustments*, and SAS No. 99, *Consideration of Fraud in a Financial Statement Audit* (AICPA, *Professional Standards*, vol. 1, AU sec. 333), establishes a requirement that an auditor, performing an audit in accordance with generally accepted auditing standards, obtain written representations for all financial statements and periods covered by the auditor's report. The Statement also provides guidance concerning the representations to be obtained, along with an illustrative management representation letter.

6.72 Land improvement and development costs generally fall within two broad classifications, permanent and limited-life, described as follows:

1. *Permanent land development costs* include the costs of initial land surveys, titles, initial clearing, and initial leveling.

2. *Limited-life land development costs* are those that will lose value as time passes or as the land and its improvements are used. Costs identified as limited-life improvements include water distribution systems, fencing, and drainage tile. The useful lives of those improvements are reasonably determinable.

Regional Differences

6.73 The nature and treatment of costs often vary in different areas of the country. For example, regional differences affect the frequency of brush removal, the useful lives of water wells, salinity control requirements and practices, and types of water conveyance systems. In some regions, deep-ripping of the soil is an initial cost that is usually not repeated. In other areas deep-ripping is required at three-to-five-year intervals.

Accounting Principles

6.74 Land development costs other than those of a recurring nature represent additions to fixed assets and should be capitalized. Permanent land development costs should not be subject to depreciation or amortization because they have an indefinite useful life. Limited-life development costs should be capitalized and depreciated over the estimated useful life of the particular improvement.

Auditing Considerations

6.75 The main audit objectives for land development costs are to obtain evidence that costs have been properly capitalized and properly classified as permanent or limited-life and that the useful lives and salvage values assigned are reasonable. Accordingly, the auditor should consider performing the following audit procedures:

1. Testing the capitalized costs by reference to cost accounting records

2. Reviewing the capitalized assets for proper classification

3. Reviewing the reasonableness of depreciation policies

Research and Development Activities

6.76 In accordance with FASB Statement No. 2, *Accounting for Research and Development Costs*, all costs related to the research and development of new and improved products should be expensed as incurred. Those costs would include the development of improved animal bloodlines or hybrid plants, trees, and vines. When this type of research and development is conducted through use of productive fields, groves, or herds, it is inappropriate to allocate costs to such newly developed breed, seed, tree, or vine types. The provisions of FASB Statement No. 2 apply when costs related to research and development of new breeds of animals or new varieties of agricultural crops are accumulated and identified.

Investments in and Transactions With Cooperatives

Investments in Cooperatives

6.77 *Background.* Investments in both supply and marketing cooperatives may consist of common or preferred stock acquired for cash and patronage allocations withheld under various capital plans. Cooperatives may issue patronage allocations through qualified notices of allocation (a taxable distribution to the patron) or through nonqualified notices of allocation (a distribution not taxable to the patron until redeemed by the cooperative). *Per-unit retains* issued by marketing cooperatives are another method of financing. (A detailed history and description of agricultural cooperatives can be found in Part 2 of this guide.)

6.78 *Accounting Principles.* Agricultural producers (patrons) should account for investments in agricultural cooperatives at cost, including allocated equities and *retains*. The carrying amount of those investments should be reduced when the cooperatives allocate losses to the patron or if the patron is unable to recover the full carrying amount of the investment.

6.79 Losses incurred by a cooperative that are not allocated to the patron may indicate such an inability on the part of the patron. At a minimum, the excess of unallocated losses over unallocated equities should be recognized by the patron on the basis of the patron's proportionate share of the total equity of the investee cooperative, or any other appropriate method, unless the patron demonstrates a likelihood that the carrying amount of the investment in the cooperative can be fully recovered.

6.80 Agricultural producers should also consider guidance provided in FASB Interpretation No. 46 (revised December 2003), *Consolidation of Variable Interest Entities* (Interpretation No. 46R), when accounting for investments in agricultural cooperatives. See paragraphs 12.20 and 12.21 for a discussion of this Interpretation.

6.81 *Auditing Considerations.* Audit procedures for investments in cooperatives are similar to those performed for other investments. The carrying amount of investments should be evaluated on the basis of records of disbursements, notices of allocation, and financial statements of the cooperatives. SAS No. 92, *Auditing Derivative Instruments, Hedging Activities, and Investments in Securities* (AICPA, *Professional Standards,* vol. 1, AU sec. 332), provides guidance on auditing investments in debt and equity securities and investments accounted for under APB Opinion No. 18. Practitioners should refer to the auditing considerations and requirements of SAS No. 92, as applicable, for the guidance. In addition, the companion Audit Guide *Auditing Derivative Instruments, Hedging Activities, and Investments in Securities,* provides practical guidance for implementing SAS No. 92.

Transactions With Cooperatives

6.82 *Background of Supply and Manufacturing Cooperatives.* Supply and manufacturing cooperatives produce or purchase goods and materials for their members. Products are generally sold to members at prices that approximate those charged at the same level of distribution by other suppliers of similar products. To the extent that sales proceeds exceed costs of goods sold and all other operating costs, the cooperatives may distribute patronage refunds. These refunds are generally based on the volume of business conducted with the cooperative and may vary by product line.

6.83 *Accounting Principles for Supply and Manufacturing Cooperatives.* Patronage refunds, in cash or equities, should either be accrued on notifications by the distributing cooperative or accrued as soon as it is probable that—

1. A refund applicable to the period will be declared.

2. One or more future events confirming the receipt of the refund are expected to occur.

3. The amount of the refund can be reasonably estimated.

4. The accrual can be made consistently from year to year.

6.84 Classification of the refunds in the financial statements should follow the recording of the costs or proceeds, or the refunds should be presented separately.

6.85 *Auditing Considerations for Supply and Manufacturing Cooperatives.* The primary objective in testing producers' transactions with supply and manufacturing cooperatives is to determine that the conditions for accrual as stated at "Accounting Principles for Supply and Manufacturing Cooperatives" (paragraphs 6.83 and 6.84) existed at the balance sheet date. Audit procedures to evaluate the reasonableness of patronage refunds to be received may include—

1. Reviewing records of refunds from previous years and considering the estimates provided by the cooperative.

2. Confirming patronage refunds receivable with the cooperative.

3. Examining patronage refund notifications.

4. Reviewing, if available, information regarding the issuing cooperative's financial position, results of operations, and cash flows.

6.86 *Background for Marketing Cooperatives.* Marketing cooperatives provide sales outlets for the products of their members and patrons. The products may be sold in a processed or unprocessed condition. For certain products there are readily determinable bases for recording exchange transactions between the cooperative and the member. Deliveries to dairy cooperatives can be recorded at market-order prices and deliveries to grain cooperatives at readily available market prices.

6.87 When marketing cooperatives operate on a pooling basis, products are usually delivered to the cooperatives for processing and sale. The identity of the product is lost upon delivery because it is commingled with products of other patrons on a multiple- or single-pool basis. The pools are *closed* (accounted for) at weekly, monthly, annual, or longer intervals. Proceeds from the sale of pooled products, less processing, marketing, and other costs of the cooperative, are returned to members of the pool, but generally some funds are retained to provide capital for the cooperative. Some processed products may not be sold for a long period of time after delivery; however, the producer generally receives advances against final settlement.

6.88 *Accounting Principles for Marketing Cooperatives.* The major accounting considerations encountered in transactions between patrons and marketing cooperatives involve the timing and method of recording the sale of products delivered. If control over the future economic benefits relative to the product has passed, ordinarily evidenced by the transfer of title, and if a reliable market price is available or the cooperative assigns a price to be paid for the product, the producer should record the delivery of product as a sale at the specified price at date of delivery. If the prior performance of the cooperative or unfavorable market conditions indicate that proceeds from the cooperative will be less than the specified price, the lower amount should be used in recording the sale.

6.89 When there is no established market price (a price determined by other market buyers or amounts assigned by the cooperative) or market prices are erratic, unstable, or volatile, the producer should treat the delivery to the cooperative as a sale at an amount equal to the accumulated cost of the product and should establish an unbilled receivable. If there are indications that the expected net proceeds will be less than cost, the unbilled receivable should be recorded at estimated net realizable value. Advances from the cooperative should be treated as reductions of the unbilled receivable and should not be used as amounts for recording sales. Variances from the amount recorded as an unbilled receivable should be recognized when reasonably determinable.

6.90 If the ultimate sales proceeds vary materially from the estimates made in the year of delivery, the financial statements should disclose the amount of current-year revenues that represent an adjustment of revenues from prior years (see APB Opinion No. 20, *Accounting Changes*, paragraph 33).

6.91 When a cooperative segregates the product delivered by the producer and accounts for it separately, and title has not been transferred, an agency relationship is created. In those situations, the producer should carry the product as inventory and record a sale only when the product has been sold by the cooperative.

6.92 Marketing cooperatives often deduct per-unit retains from the estimated proceeds due producers. Per-unit retains are based on the quantity of product delivered by the producer and are a method of financing for the cooperative. For producers, the retains represent investments in the cooperative. Producers should record the per-unit retains at face value and, if the retains are not to be redeemed in the current year, they should be classified as noncurrent.

6.93 Accruals of patronage refunds from marketing cooperatives should follow the principles stated in "Accounting Principles for Supply and Manufacturing Cooperatives," paragraphs 6.83 and 6.84.

6.94 When a producer is economically dependent on a cooperative for sale of all or a significant portion of annual production, the extent of such transactions should be disclosed in the financial statements.

6.95 *Auditing Considerations for Marketing Cooperatives.* The primary audit objective in testing producers' transactions with marketing cooperatives is to obtain evidence regarding the propriety of the amount recognized as a sale at the time the product is delivered to the cooperative. Audit procedures may include—

1. For products with reliable market prices, testing the reasonableness of sales amounts by reference to quoted prices adjusted for estimated marketing and distribution costs to be deducted by the cooperative.

2. Confirming receivables from the cooperative.

3. Examining cash receipts from the cooperative.

4. Inspecting correspondence from the cooperative.

5. Inspecting bills of lading and weight tickets.

Government Loans and Agricultural Programs

Loan Programs

6.96 Under various stabilization programs, producers of certain crops or products may receive federal agency loans that are collateralized by security interests in negotiable warehouse receipts. The producer is not required to repay the loans but may relinquish title to the stored crop or product to satisfy the obligation. Because the producer has title to the product until a decision is made to liquidate the obligation by transfer of title to the lender, the loan should be shown in total as a current liability and the inventory recorded as an asset. Conditions may exist where the net realizable value of the commodity is less than the loan and accrued interest. In those cases the net realizable value of the commodity should be equal to the loan, including accrued interest. SAS No. 1, section 331.14, as amended by SAS No. 43, discusses controls and auditing procedures for goods stored in public warehouses.

Income Replacement and Subsidy Programs

6.97 Income replacement and subsidy programs are designed to bring income from commodities to certain predetermined levels and include—

- Deficiency payments, which are subsidy payments resulting from low prices for designated commodities.
- Disaster payments, which may be made to producers when disasters prevent planting or reduce yields on crops.
- Other programs, which are available to producers to encourage production, provide indemnity for certain types of losses, and reimburse producers for withholding land from production.

Existing programs change periodically, and it may be necessary to know their current status on a particular audit engagement. Information regarding these programs can be obtained from offices of the Agricultural Stabilization and Conservation Service, United States Department of Agriculture.

6.98 All of the above payments, while different in nature, constitute additional income and should be recorded when the amount of and right to receive the payment can be reasonably determined.

Cost-Sharing Programs

6.99 Under cost-sharing programs, the government reimburses producers or shares the cost of certain expenditures with them. Such programs include reimbursement for weed control and cost-sharing of expenditures for ditch lining, earthen dams, and prevention of soil erosion.

6.100 Reimbursements of costs for capital expenditures should be accumulated and applied against the total fixed asset costs. Direct payments by the government agency should be accounted for as if the producer had received the payment and made the expenditure. Reimbursements of expense items should be applied to reduce the recorded amount of the expenses. The payments should be recorded in the period when the original expenditure occurred, unless it is not practicable to estimate the amount of the reimbursement or determine eligibility for the benefit.

Income Taxes

6.101 Most agricultural producers receive special treatment under income tax laws, including the right to elect to use the cash method of accounting, the right to use certain inventory valuation methods that are not in accordance with generally accepted accounting principles, and the right to currently deduct certain expenditures for items of a capital nature. As a consequence, many transactions affect the determination of pretax accounting income in one period and the computation of taxable income in another reporting period. Those transactions create temporary differences that require the recognition of deferred tax liabilities and assets in the financial statements.

6.102 The provisions of FASB Statement No. 109, *Accounting for Income Taxes*, are applicable to agricultural enterprises. FASB Statement No. 109 establishes financial accounting and reporting standards for the effects of income taxes that result from an enterprise's activities during the current and preceding years. It requires an asset and liability approach for financial accounting and reporting for income taxes.

6.103 In accordance with the provisions of FASB Statement No. 109, the following basic principles are applied in accounting for income taxes at the date of the financial statements—

- *a.* A current tax liability or asset is recognized for the estimated taxes payable or refundable on tax returns for the current year.

- *b.* A deferred tax liability or asset is recognized for the estimated future tax effects attributable to temporary differences and carryforwards.

- *c.* The measurement of current and deferred tax liabilities and assets is based on provisions of the enacted tax law; the effects of future changes in tax laws or rates are not anticipated.

- *d.* The measurement of deferred tax assets is reduced, if necessary, by the amount of any tax benefits that, based on available evidence, are not expected to be realized.

PART II—Agricultural Cooperatives

Chapter 7

Introduction

History

7.01 The genesis of the modern cooperative movement is generally attributed to the first consumer cooperative organized in 1844 by a small group of laborers in Rochdale, Lancashire, England. The following principles were developed in that first cooperative: (1) sale for cash and not on credit, (2) charges that matched prevailing local prices, (3) refunds in proportion to purchases, (4) limited interest on capital investments, (5) one vote for each member, and (6) regular and frequent meetings.

7.02 The emergence of the cooperative movement in the United States came in 1875, when the so-called Rochdale principles were formally adopted at a convention of the National Grange (an organization of farmers). By 1900, a substantial number of these farmer-owned organizations were in operation, and although most of them were small they were beginning to exert an influence on the agricultural economy of the nation. Since that early beginning, cooperatives have grown in size and number. In 1985, there were about 5,600 agricultural cooperatives in the United States with about 4.7 million farmer members.

7.03 Congress has encouraged the development of agricultural cooperatives through favorable legislation, including—
- Special rules that soften or nullify the effect of antitrust laws.
- Recognition of the cooperative's nonprofit nature by allowing patrons' qualifying distributions to be excluded from taxable income of the cooperative.

Organizational Characteristics and Functions

7.04 Agricultural cooperatives engage in a variety of activities that include—
- food processing and distribution
- oil production and refining
- manufacturing
- transportation
- research

7.05 Cooperatives are not identified by any particular activity, but rather by their form of organization. The basic characteristics of cooperatives are summarized as follows:

1. Most agricultural cooperatives are organized as corporations, but they may or may not issue capital stock. Cooperatives differ from other corporations in that the net earnings of cooperatives are allocated to patrons on a patronage basis rather than to members on the basis of equities held. Dividends paid on stock or membership capital are usually limited.

2. Cooperatives are owned and controlled by their members, generally based on the one-member-one-vote principle or limited-weighted voting, regardless of the amount of stock or membership capital owned.

3. To be recognized as a cooperative for federal income tax purposes, an organization must operate on a cooperative basis. To qualify as a tax-exempt cooperative, to borrow from the banks for cooperatives, and to qualify for exemption from registration under the federal securities acts, a cooperative must meet quantitative requirements relating to the value of business done with members.

4. Except for a few large organizations, cooperatives do not have substantial amounts of nonpatron capital. Typically, cooperatives are organized with small amounts of original capital, and equity is accumulated by retaining allocated earnings and issuing qualified or nonqualified written notices of allocation to patrons.* Capital may also be accumulated by retaining after-tax patronage and nonpatronage earnings.

5. The federal income tax status of agricultural cooperatives is an important characteristic. Section 521 of the Internal Revenue Code provides a limited tax exemption for certain cooperatives.

Because of the requirements necessary to maintain exempt status under section 521, many cooperatives operate as nonexempt cooperative organizations. The rules for taxation of both exempt and nonexempt cooperatives are set forth in subchapter T of the Internal Revenue Code, sections 1381 through 1388. The requirements for exempt status under section 521 and some of the provisions of subchapter T are outlined in chapter 8 of this guide.

---

* In May 2003, the FASB issued FASB Statement of Financial Accounting Standards No. 150, *Accounting for Certain Financial Instruments With Characteristics of Both Liabilities and Equity*. This Statement establishes standards for how an issuer classifies and measures certain financial instruments with characteristics of both liabilities and equity. It requires that an issuer classify a financial instrument that is within its scope as a liability (or an asset in some circumstances). Many of those instruments were previously classified as equity.

This Standard may have a significant impact on financial statements of agricultural cooperatives. Retained allocated equities which are usually repaid to cooperative patrons over a specific number of years generally meet the definition of mandatorily redeemable financial instruments under FASB Statement No. 150 and as such may have to be reclassified as liabilities. As a result, some agricultural cooperatives may report significantly reduced equities and increased liabilities in their GAAP financial statements.

In November 2003, the FASB issued FASB Staff Position (FSP) FAS 150-3, which defers the effective date of the mandatorily redeemable provisions of FASB Statement No. 150 and all related FSPs for nonpublic entities as follows: (*a*) until fiscal periods beginning after December 15, 2004 for instruments that are mandatorily redeemable on fixed dates and (*b*) indefinitely, pending further FASB action, if the redemption date is not fixed or if the payout amount is variable and not based on an index. Readers should be alert to further developments.

Chapter 8

Background Information

Types of Cooperative Organizations and Services

8.01 Agricultural cooperatives may be classified by their operational characteristics in the following manner:

1. Marketing cooperatives market agricultural products for patrons in unprocessed and processed condition. Products typically marketed include milk, fruits, vegetables, nuts, livestock, poultry, eggs, grain, wool, and cotton. Marketing cooperatives range in size from small country grain elevators to very large organizations with nationally advertised brands. Most marketing cooperatives take title to patrons' products and process or pack them for sale to wholesale or retail customers. Other cooperatives act as agents for their patrons on a commission or brokerage basis.

2. Bargaining cooperatives negotiate with packers and processors, provide market information, and act as intermediaries between their patrons and packers and processors.

3. Supply or purchasing cooperatives purchase, manufacture, distribute, and provide feed, petroleum products, fertilizer, chemicals, farm supplies, and services of various kinds to their patrons. Supply cooperatives range in size from very small local retail units to large regional manufacturing and wholesale organizations. Most small retail cooperatives purchase the equipment and supplies sold to their patrons from large regional cooperatives or other trade sources. Many large regional cooperatives operate manufacturing facilities for the production of various products and supplies. The facilities may be operated independently or in association with other large regional cooperatives.

4. Service cooperatives provide artificial insemination, breeding of livestock, data processing, equipment leasing, insurance, financing, and other services to agricultural producers.

8.02 Large regional cooperatives, as well as many small cooperatives, may engage in both marketing and supply activities. Grain marketing cooperatives, for example, often sell feed, fertilizer, and farm supplies to patrons.

Relationships With Members and Patrons

8.03 The members of a cooperative are usually its patrons. (As defined in the Glossary, the terms *members* and *patrons* are often used interchangeably.) There is a unique relationship between the cooperative and its members and patrons. The cooperative performs marketing, supply, or other services for its patrons and usually agrees to distribute to them, on a patronage basis, any revenues in excess of costs that it derives from performing those services. In some nonexempt cooperatives a patron must also be a member to receive a distribution.

8.04 An underlying concept of cooperative ownership and operation is the equitable treatment of patrons. This is particularly significant for cooperatives claiming exempt status under section 521 of the Internal Revenue Code. Cooperatives may be denied tax-exempt status if they do not deal with member and nonmember patrons on an equitable basis. Equitable treatment in the allocation of net earnings among patrons is also important for *non*-exempt cooperatives, because it is generally required in order to maintain cooperative status under the federal income tax laws. Cooperatives' eligibility to borrow from various banks for cooperatives may also be affected by inequitable treatment of patrons. In addition, failure to treat patrons equitably may subject a cooperative to litigation by patrons.

8.05 After cooperatives have provided supplies or other services or performed marketing functions for their patrons, they generally allocate revenues in excess of costs from those activities on a patronage basis. This excess is referred to as *net margins, net proceeds, net savings,* or *net earnings.* In the discussion that follows, the more frequent use of the terms *earnings* or *net earnings* is not intended to imply preferability. Regardless of the terminology used, allocation of earnings must be made on an equitable and consistent basis.

8.06 Generally, the earnings of cooperatives are classified as either *patronage* or *nonpatronage.* The excess of revenues over costs resulting from transactions for or with patrons is *patronage* source earnings.

8.07 *Nonpatronage* earnings result from transactions other than those with or for patrons. Examples are nonpatronage income from investments in securities, rental income from nonpatronage activities, and income earned on sales or purchases made on a nonpatronage basis. It is sometimes difficult to distinguish between patronage and nonpatronage earnings, especially when patronage and nonpatronage activities overlap. However, distinguishing between the two types of earnings is very important because of the tax treatment of patronage source income.

8.08 Allocations of net earnings to patrons are called *patronage refunds, patronage dividends*, or *patronage distributions.* These allocations may be made in cash or in a combination of cash and *equity certificates.* Equity certificates, such as revolving-fund certificates and capital certificates, are credited to the individual patron's account and are usually revolved (paid) over a period of years. Revolvement practices may be defined in governance documents such as bylaws or may be specified by the board policy. Revolvement may be linked to the date of issue (e.g., revolvement on a FIFO basis) or may be linked to some other benchmark, such as the patron's attained age, the patron's retirement from farming, etc. Bylaws frequently spell out that revolvement is strictly at the discretion of the board of directors. The proportion of refunds to be distributed as cash and equity certificates and the revolving period of these certificates are specified in the cooperative's bylaws or determined by its board of directors.[*]

---

[*] In May 2003, the FASB issued FASB Statement of Financial Accounting Standards No. 150, *Accounting for Certain Financial Instruments With Characteristics of Both Liabilities and Equity.* This Statement establishes standards for how an issuer classifies and measures certain financial instruments with characteristics of both liabilities and equity. It requires that an issuer classify a financial instrument that is within its scope as a liability (or an asset in some circumstances). Many of those instruments were previously classified as equity.

This Standard may have a significant impact on financial statements of agricultural cooperatives. Retained allocated equities which are usually repaid to cooperative patrons over a specific number of years generally meet the definition of mandatorily redeemable financial instruments under FASB Statement No. 150 and as such may have to be reclassified as liabilities. As a result, some agricultural cooperatives may report significantly reduced equities and increased liabilities in their GAAP financial statements.

In November 2003, the FASB issued FASB Staff Position (FSP) FAS 150-3, which defers the effective date of the mandatorily redeemable provisions of FASB Statement No. 150 and all related FSPs for nonpublic entities as follows: (a) until fiscal periods beginning after December 15, 2004 for instruments that are mandatorily redeemable on fixed dates and (b) indefinitely, pending further FASB action, if the redemption date is not fixed or if the payout amount is variable and not based on an index. Readers should be alert to further developments.

Related-Party Transactions

8.09 The underlying concept of cooperatives is ownership and control by members and patrons with and for whom cooperatives conduct their operations. It is common for patrons, officers, and directors to own or have interests in enterprises that transact business with the cooperatives. Accordingly, cooperatives are involved in related-party transactions as a result of their normal activities. When related-party transactions are material, disclosure should be made in accordance with FASB Statement No. 57, *Related Party Disclosures.*

Federal Income Taxes and Cooperative Operations

8.10 Internal Revenue Code section 521 provides a limited exemption for associations of farmers organized and operated as cooperatives for either (1) marketing the producers' products and returning the net earnings to them on the basis of either quantity or value of the products furnished or (2) purchasing supplies and equipment for use by the members or other persons and returning the net earnings to them on the basis of the purchases made.

8.11 Before 1951, cooperatives described in Internal Revenue Code section 521 were not subject to income taxes. Income taxes, if any, were paid at the patron level. In 1951 legislation was passed to ensure that cooperative earnings would be currently taxable to either the cooperatives or the patrons. However, court decisions have generally held that, under the 1951 Act, noncash allocations of patronage were not taxable to the patron even though they were deductible by the cooperatives.

8.12 Subchapter T of the Internal Revenue Code (sections 1381 through 1388) was enacted in 1962 to resolve this situation. It provided the first statutory recognition for the patronage distributions of nonexempt cooperatives and continued the tax treatment previously available to exempt cooperatives with respect to nonpatronage distributions and dividends on capital stock. The principal change introduced by subchapter T was to limit deductions for cooperative distributions to amounts that patrons individually consent to recognize as income for tax purposes.

8.13 The criteria necessary for an organization to qualify under section 521 follow:

1. The dividend rate on the capital stock may not exceed the legal rate of interest in the state of incorporation or 8 percent per year, whichever is greater.

2. Substantially all capital stock (other than nonvoting preferred stock) must be owned by the producers that market their products or purchase their supplies and equipment through the cooperative.

3. Owners of nonvoting preferred stock are not permitted by virtue of their stock ownership to participate directly or indirectly in cooperative earnings beyond fixed dividends.

4. Products marketed for nonmembers by a marketing cooperative may not exceed the value of products marketed for members.

5. The value of supplies and equipment purchased by a supply cooperative for nonmembers may not exceed the value of supplies and equipment purchased for members, provided the value of purchases made for persons who are neither members nor producers generally does not exceed 15 percent of the value of all purchases.

6. Business done for the U.S. government or any of its agencies is disregarded in determining the right to exemption.

8.14 If a cooperative is exempt under section 521, it obtains two deductions in addition to those allowed cooperatives in general:

1. Limited amounts paid as dividends on capital stock during the taxable year

2. Amounts of nonpatronage earnings paid or allocated on a patronage basis to patrons within eight-and-one-half months after the close of the taxable year

8.15 Internal Revenue Code sections 1381 through 1388 and related regulations prescribe the tax treatment for cooperatives. In general, these sections apply to all cooperatives except rural electric and telephone cooperatives, although certain portions apply only to exempt cooperatives.

8.16 Internal Revenue Code sections 1381 through 1388 impose a tax on all cooperative net earnings that are not distributed to patrons in cash or qualified written notices of allocation. These sections enable exempt and nonexempt cooperatives to avail themselves of tax deductions for patronage distributions and also permit exempt cooperatives to deduct distributions of nonpatronage income and dividends on capital. The tax treatment for the recipients is also covered in these sections.

8.17 For patronage distributions to be treated as qualified allocations, at least 20 percent of the distribution must be paid in cash. The noncash portion of the allocation must be in the form of a qualified written notice of allocation and must be furnished to the patron within eight-and-one-half months after the end of the fiscal year of the cooperative. The patrons must agree, either in writing or through bylaw consent, to include the amount of the qualified written notice of allocation, together with the cash received, in taxable income in the year of receipt.

8.18 Cooperatives may issue nonqualified written notices of allocation and recognize income tax at the cooperative level. Upon redemption of nonqualified notices of allocation, the issuing cooperatives are entitled to a current tax credit for taxes paid in the year of origination of the nonqualified notices of allocation or a deduction for the amount of the nonqualified notices redeemed, for the year of origination or the year of redemption, whichever provides the issuing cooperative the greater tax benefit.

8.19 Per-unit retains withheld from patrons of marketing cooperatives are generally based on units of products delivered or on some other unit or percentage basis rather than on earnings. They may be issued on a qualified or nonqualified basis. Qualified per-unit retains are deductible by the cooperative for income tax purposes but nonqualified per-unit retains are not. The rules governing the issuance of per-unit retains are similar to those applicable to patronage refunds, except a minimum payment of 20 percent in cash is not required for per-unit retains issued on a qualified basis.

8.20 Many marketing cooperatives, for processing and marketing purposes, commingle agricultural products into a pool. The products are treated as a unit, and each pool patron receives an equitable share of net earnings from the pool. Some pools may be held open beyond the end of the fiscal year. In those instances earnings for patronage-refund purposes are recognized in the year the pool is closed (Internal Revenue Code section 1382[e]).

Regulatory Commissions

8.21 Most cooperatives do not issue to third parties the type of debt and equity instruments that are subject to the registration provisions of the

Securities Act of 1933. The specific exemptions given to farmer cooperative organizations are found in section 3 of the Act and include any security issued by an agricultural cooperative exempt from tax under Internal Revenue Code section 521. However, certain securities of nonexempt cooperatives are subject to the provisions of the Securities Act of 1933.

8.22 The Securities Exchange Act of 1934, on the other hand, exempts substantially all agricultural cooperatives from its section 12(g) registration provisions, related annual and periodic reporting, and proxy and insider trading requirements.

8.23 Cooperatives are, to some extent, exempt from antitrust prosecution by the Federal Trade Commission under the Capper-Volstead Act. As cooperatives grow in size and influence, there are continuous challenges to this exemption from the monopoly and restraint-of-trade rules contained in the Sherman and Clayton Acts. Section 2 of the Capper-Volstead Act gives the secretary of agriculture the power to prevent cooperatives from using monopoly power for "undue price enhancement."

Market Orders and Government Support Programs

8.24 Marketing cooperatives may be affected by federal and state market orders and support programs for products such as milk, fresh fruits and vegetables, grains, dried fruits, and nuts. Marketing orders are usually initiated by the producers of an agricultural commodity in an attempt to stabilize the market and assure an adequate return. If the secretary of agriculture or the appropriate state agencies agree it is needed, an order legally obligating commodity handlers to comply with specified trade practices and sales restrictions is issued.

8.25 Market orders may restrict the quality, size, or grade of the commodity to be marketed. Specific provisions of market orders vary. Some orders apply to the entire U.S. production of a commodity, whereas others apply only to production in certain areas. Some orders limit the absolute quantity that can be marketed, whereas others limit only the quantity in certain markets (fresh or processed, for example) or the amount that can be marketed at certain times of the year.

8.26 Cooperatives may participate in government support programs (the Commodity Credit Corporation) on behalf of their members. This participation requires special segregation of sales proceeds, inventories, interest expense, and other amounts for the commodities covered by the programs.

Chapter 9

Engagement Planning for Agricultural Cooperatives[*]

9.01 SAS No. 22 provides general guidance for planning an audit engagement. There are several planning considerations significant to the audit of agricultural cooperatives, including—

- The method of accounting for unprocessed products delivered by patrons of marketing cooperatives, including the basis for assigned amounts if they are used.
- The valuation of inventories of finished products in marketing cooperatives operating on a pooling basis.
- The board of directors' intentions regarding redemptions of equities and retains.[**]
- The existence of forward and futures contracts and other derivatives.
- The methods of allocation of gains and losses to various pools.
- Timing and amounts of advances against estimated pool proceeds.
- The need for services of a specialist to evaluate the quality of the cooperative's inventories (see SAS No. 73).
- Government and tax regulations that affect cooperatives' activities.

---

[*] Auditors of issuers need to refer to the Preface of this Guide for important information related to the PCAOB.

[**] In May 2003, the FASB issued FASB Statement of Financial Accounting Standards No. 150, *Accounting for Certain Financial Instruments With Characteristics of Both Liabilities and Equity.* This Statement establishes standards for how an issuer classifies and measures certain financial instruments with characteristics of both liabilities and equity. It requires that an issuer classify a financial instrument that is within its scope as a liability (or an asset in some circumstances). Many of those instruments were previously classified as equity.

This Standard may have a significant impact on financial statements of agricultural cooperatives. Retained allocated equities, including retains, which are usually repaid to cooperative patrons over a specific number of years generally meet the definition of mandatorily redeemable financial instruments under FASB Statement No. 150 and as such may have to be reclassified as liabilities. As a result, some agricultural cooperatives may report significantly reduced equities and increased liabilities in their GAAP financial statements.

In November 2003, the FASB issued FASB Staff Position (FSP) FAS 150-3, which defers the effective date of the mandatorily redeemable provisions of FASB Statement No. 150 and all related FSPs for nonpublic entities as follows: (*a*) until fiscal periods beginning after December 15, 2004 for instruments that are mandatorily redeemable on fixed dates and (*b*) indefinitely, pending further FASB action, if the redemption date is not fixed or if the payout amount is variable and not based on an index. Readers should be alert to further developments.

Chapter 10

Special Accounting and Auditing Considerations[*] [**]

Accounting by Marketing Cooperatives Operating on a Pooling Basis

Background and Unique Characteristics

10.01 Because specific product identification is not practical for marketing patrons' products that must be commingled and processed before they are sold, cooperatives generally have adopted the *pool* method of accounting for these products. Under that method cooperatives take title to the patrons' products on delivery, commingle products of like kind and grade, and sell the finished products for their own account. Records of sales, payments for products, and costs are maintained for each pool. When the pool is closed, the net proceeds are distributed to members of the pool, based on the amounts assigned to the products provided by each patron.

10.02 Accounting periods for pools vary from a week to longer than a year, based on the production and marketing cycle. Short pool periods are used for products such as eggs, which have a short production and marketing cycle. Longer pool periods are often necessary for such products as canned fruits and vegetables that require more than one year to process and market.

10.03 Both single- and multiple-pool methods of accounting are used by marketing cooperatives to allocate net proceeds to pools:

10.04 *Single-Pool Method.* Net proceeds from operations are allocated to patrons on a proportional basis, usually based on the amounts assigned to the products delivered to the cooperative.

---

[*] The effective dates of FASB Statements No. 141, *Business Combinations*, and No. 142, *Goodwill and Other Intangible Assets*, were deferred for combinations between two or more mutual enterprises (cooperatives are mutual enterprises) to allow the FASB time to consider whether there are any unique attributes of mutual enterprises to justify an accounting treatment different from that provided in those Statements. That means that mutual enterprises will continue to account for business combinations and acquired intangible assets following the guidance in APB Opinion No. 16, *Business Combinations*, and APB Opinion No. 17, *Intangible Assets*, until a final Statement on combinations of mutual enterprises is issued and effective.

The FASB's tentative decisions reached in the *Combinations Between Mutual Enterprises* project will be included in the Exposure Draft for the *Business Combinations: Purchase Methods Procedures* project which is expected to be issued in the second quarter of 2004. This project uses a "differences-based" approach that presumes that the provisions of FASB Statements No. 141 and No. 142 apply to combinations between mutual enterprises, unless conditions of the combination are found to be so different as to warrant a different accounting treatment. The most notable of those differences identified are the lack of equity investors (in the traditional sense) and the lack of a readily identifiable and measurable monetary consideration.

If adopted as proposed, the FASB's decisions on combinations between two or more mutual enterprises should be applied to combinations occurring in fiscal years beginning after December 15, 2004 and interim periods within those fiscal years. The FASB decided to amend FASB Statement No. 142 to remove the delayed effectiveness provisions for combinations between mutual enterprises—the provisions of that Statement (including its transition provisions) would apply to mutual enterprises for fiscal years beginning after the date that a final Statement is issued. More information on this project is available on FASB Web site at www.fasb.org.

[**] Auditors of issuers need to refer to the Preface of this Guide for important information related to the PCAOB.

10.05 *Multiple-Pool Method.* Products received are accounted for in separate product pools. Net proceeds of the separate pools are allocated to patrons of those pools usually based on the amounts assigned to the products delivered to the cooperative.

Accounting Principles

10.06 Overhead allocations to product lines are unnecessary when the single-pool method is used. This allows the management of marketing cooperatives with several departments, such as canning, freezing, or fresh shipping, more flexibility in determining alternative levels of production.

10.07 The following example illustrates pool settlement under multiple- and single-pool methods:

Product	Unprocessed Product Assigned Amounts	Percent	Net Proceeds Allocated to Patrons			
			Multiple-Pool		Single-Pool	
			Amount	Percent	Amount	Percent
A	$ 5,000	50	$ 700	70	$ 500	50
B	2,000	20	100	10	200	20
C	3,000	30	200	20	300	30
Total	$10,000	100	$1,000	100	$1,000	100

In this example, the allocation of net proceeds to patrons under the multiple-pool method was determined by the separate accounting for the operations of each product (each product is a separate pool); therefore, the percentages differ from the unprocessed product percentages. Under the single-pool method, the net proceeds from total operations are allocated on the basis of the value of the unprocessed product and the percentages are the same as the unprocessed product percentages.

10.08 If the production and marketing cycle extends beyond one year, marketing cooperatives may have substantial inventories of finished goods on hand at the end of the fiscal year. Marketing cooperatives often transfer (in effect, "sell") such inventories to the succeeding year's pools, thus allowing the current pools to be closed on an annual basis. This method is often used when the type and quantity of products delivered by members do not vary materially from year to year. Other cooperatives hold the pools open beyond one year and do not close them until substantially all the pooled inventories have been sold.

10.09 Accounting for overall losses is a difficult problem for both single- and multiple-pool operations. In addition, multiple-pool operations may be faced with the problem of disposing of losses from individual pools. Accounting for those losses is addressed in the "Accounting for Losses" and "Departmental and Functional Accounting" sections that follow in paragraphs 10.12 through 10.19, respectively.

10.10 Although the preceding paragraphs relate primarily to marketing cooperatives, supply cooperatives encounter similar problems in allocating earnings to members, particularly if both manufacturing and distribution are involved. Patrons of supply cooperatives buy goods and services at approximately the same prices that would be paid to other suppliers. Earnings are determined periodically and allocated to patrons on the basis of the business done by each patron with the cooperative.

Auditing Considerations

10.11   The auditor should consider performing the following procedures when auditing the determination and allocation of pool proceeds:

1. Obtaining an understanding of controls over the system of recording sales, cost of sales, and expenses

2. Reviewing pool closings and allocations of pool proceeds, including advances, made during the year, as well as those made after year-end but before the date of the auditor's report

3. Testing the pool closings and allocation of pool proceeds to patrons for—
    - Clerical accuracy
    - Compliance with the board of directors' actions
    - Compliance with the cooperative's bylaws
    - Compliance with tax regulations
    - Compliance with established accounting policies
    - Consistency of application from pool period to pool period

Accounting for Losses

Background

10.12   A cooperative may incur an overall loss in a given year. The disposition of losses may be made based on bylaws or the board of directors' action.

Accounting Principles

10.13   Cooperatives use a number of different methods for disposing of an overall loss, including—

1. Allocating the loss to patrons on the basis of current patronage. The loss may offset the patrons' equities, future patronage allocations, or future cash contributions.

2. Allocating the loss to all equities without considering current patronage. However, patrons with substantial equities and decreasing patronage may be treated inequitably if this method is used.

3. Charging the loss to unallocated retained earnings. This method is equitable when the loss is attributable to nonpatronage business.

4. Offsetting the loss against amounts available for patronage allocation in subsequent years before making any such allocation to patrons. This method may be acceptable if the patrons are substantially the same from year to year.

Auditing Considerations

10.14   The auditor should perform the following procedures in reviewing the disposition of overall operating losses of cooperatives:

1. Reading those sections of the bylaws and articles of incorporation describing the procedures for disposition of losses

2. Reviewing the board of directors' minutes to determine policies or actions for allocation of losses

3. Reviewing the method of allocating losses to determine that the method is in accordance with the cooperative's bylaws or board actions

4. Testing the mathematical accuracy of allocated losses

5. Reviewing allocations made during the year under audit and those made after the balance sheet date up until the report date

Departmental and Functional Accounting

Background and Unique Characteristics

10.15 Cooperatives operating on a functional or departmental basis may have net earnings from one function or department and operating losses from another. It is a common practice for losses from one function or department to be absorbed by profits from another function or department before earnings to patrons are allocated. Some cooperatives distribute departmental earnings to patrons and charge departmental losses to unallocated retained earnings. The method of accounting for functional or departmental earnings and losses, and the basis for making allocations to patrons, may be provided for in the bylaws or by actions of the board of directors.

Accounting Principles

10.16 To allocate earnings to patrons equitably, cooperatives usually account for revenues and costs by function (supply or marketing) or departments within the function.

10.17 Expenses common to one or more functions or departments should be allocated on a reasonable and consistent basis. In addition, one department of a cooperative may handle several commodities, and departmental revenues and expenses may have to be allocated among them.

10.18 Cooperatives may incur a loss in one department or function and realize earnings in another. Methods of accounting for these departmental and functional losses include—

1. Offsetting the losses of unprofitable departments against profitable ones, and allocating the remaining profit to the patrons of the profitable departments by using the allocation method adopted by the cooperative.

2. Recovering the loss from the patrons of that department or function on the basis of bylaw provisions or a marketing agreement.

3. Subtracting the loss from net nonpatronage income. Offsetting patronage losses against nonpatronage income may not eliminate the income tax due on the nonpatronage income of a nonexempt cooperative.

4. Charging the loss to unallocated retained earnings, and allocating income from profitable departments or functions to patrons on the basis of the cooperative's allocation methods.

5. Offsetting the losses against patronage allocation for subsequent years prior to making departmental and functional allocations to patrons.

Auditing Considerations

10.19 The auditor should understand the process of accounting for functional or departmental results and the allocation of net earnings to patrons, and should also consider the following additional procedures for functional or departmental operations:

1. Obtaining an understanding of controls over the generation of information on a functional or departmental basis, including sales, direct costs, and the allocation of common costs by department and commodity

2. Reviewing the allocation of overhead costs for consistency and compliance with governing documents and board actions

3. Reviewing the methods for allocating departmental losses for compliance with governing documents and board actions

4. Reviewing allocations made during the year under audit and those made after the balance sheet date up until the report date

Chapter 11

Specific Accounting Principles and Auditing Considerations*

Inventories

Background and Unique Characteristics

11.01 Inventory methods of cooperatives encompass a wide range of practices. Supply cooperatives generally have a reliable purchase price for inventories on hand. Many marketing cooperatives have a known or determinable market price on which to base amounts to be paid for patrons' products. However, some marketing cooperatives operating on a pooling basis do not have a reliable market price on which to value and account for receipt of patrons' products.

Accounting Principles

11.02 Selecting a method to account for product inventories depends on the financial information available, marketing agreements, bylaws, and actions of the board of directors. A discussion of accounting for product inventories at lower of cost or market and net realizable value follows. (Also see paragraphs 83 to 86 in SOP 85-3 [appendix C].)

11.03 *Net-Realizable-Value Method.* Some marketing cooperatives operating on a pooling basis cannot determine the market price of patrons' products when received because a reliable price for the products is not available. Such cooperatives usually process and market a high percentage of limited specialty crops. Many of those cooperatives account for inventories of goods in process and finished goods at net realizable value, determined by deducting estimated completion and disposition costs from the estimated sales price of the processed inventory. Furthermore, many processing cooperatives use net realizable value for product inventories in order to comply with bylaw provisions and contractual obligations and to facilitate equitable pool settlements from pool period to pool period and among various classes of patrons. If inventories are accounted for at net realizable value, there should be a corresponding effect on earnings and amounts due patrons. The entity's involvement with derivative instruments and hedging activities may also need to be considered.

11.04 The calculation of net realizable value for product inventories requires the determination of sales dates, sales prices, and the estimated costs of completion and disposal. The sales prices may be based on comparable sales or published market prices.

11.05 *Lower of Cost or Market Method.* Inventories of supply, manufacturing, and other service cooperatives present no unusual accounting problems and are usually accounted for at the lower of cost or market on a FIFO, LIFO, or average-cost basis.

11.06 Marketing cooperatives, such as grain and dairy cooperatives, that receive products from patrons and pay their patrons a firm market price at time of delivery or shortly thereafter, regardless of the amount of the cooperative's

---

* Auditors of issuers need to refer to the Preface of this Guide for important information related to the PCAOB.

earnings, should treat the payments as purchases. Those cooperatives have established costs and can determine inventories at the lower of cost or market, with cost determined on a FIFO, LIFO, or average-cost basis.

11.07 Boards of directors of marketing cooperatives that operate on a pooling basis with no obligation to pay patrons fixed prices may assign to patrons' products amounts that approximate estimated market. These assigned amounts are cost and should be charged to cost of production and credited to amounts due patrons. Inventories are then accounted for at the lower of cost or market. However, some cooperatives may value the inventories at net realizable value to facilitate determination of pool proceeds.

Auditing Considerations

11.08 Tests of inventory quantities and quality are generally the same as those applied in the audits of other commercial entities. To test the calculation of lower of cost or market or net realizable value, the auditor should consider—

1. Testing inventory costs by—
   - Comparing amounts paid to patrons or assigned to patrons' products with market prices paid by others or prices established by the board.
   - Reviewing additional processing and packaging costs for reasonableness and consistency.
   - Reviewing variances between actual and standard costs for reasonableness and consistency.
2. Testing net realizable value, which is calculated in essentially the same way as market for inventories valued at the lower of cost or market, by—
   - Reviewing price lists and actual sales at and subsequent to the valuation date.
   - Testing sales prices by referring to available prices for similar products of other processors.
   - Reviewing marketability of various groups of finished-product inventories on the basis of existing market conditions.
   - Reviewing open orders to determine future sales prices.
   - Determining that disposal costs include normal shipping, storage, selling, and production overhead costs.
   - Testing computation of completion and disposal costs for reasonableness and consistency.
3. Testing the lower-of-cost-or-market calculations by comparing net realizable values with cost and determining that writedowns have been consistently recognized on a line-by-line, a commodity-by-commodity, or an overall basis.
4. Reviewing the mix of finished goods to be packed from those inventories if bulk and in-process inventories are to be valued at net realizable value, comparing the projected mix with prior experience for reasonableness, and considering a writedown of any excess inventory quantities.

11.09 In the audit of product-delivery transactions between patrons and cooperatives operating on a pooling basis, the auditor should consider—

1. Reviewing the reasonableness of the amounts assigned to patrons' products by comparing the amounts with values for products obtained from established markets, bargaining-association contracts, and federal and state crop-reporting services.

2. Selecting patron statements on a test basis and—
   - Reviewing approval of patrons' product prices.
   - Testing the accuracy of extensions and footings.
   - Comparing the amounts due patrons with subsequent payments.
   - Comparing quantities delivered by patrons with weight tickets.
   - Comparing deductions for freight and other expenses with approved deduction schedules.

3. Comparing statements to determine that patrons receive similar treatment and terms.

4. Confirming directly with patrons the quantity of products delivered, payments received, and equity balances.

5. Determining whether retains are recorded correctly as an element of equity if per-unit retains are deducted from patrons' products payments.[*]

6. Determining whether payments to patrons are made in accordance with written agreements and whether all parties have complied with all the terms.

7. Determining whether payments to nonmembers are made in accordance with established policies and rates.

Investments in Other Cooperatives

Background and Unique Characteristics

11.10 Agricultural cooperatives may join and invest in one or more other cooperatives to purchase farm-related products, to process and market farm products, or to obtain financing. The investments are long-term in nature and are an extension of the cooperative's own productive facilities and capital. In most instances, voting rights accompanying these investments are based on the one-member-one-vote principle or are limited to weighted voting based on patronage rather than on the amount of the investment. The sale of such investments to parties other than the issuer is often restricted or prohibited. Accordingly, such investments are made primarily to obtain the benefits offered by the cooperative rather than for investment or capital-appreciation purposes.

11.11 Investments in agricultural cooperatives may include initial cash commitments for common and preferred stock, subsequent per-unit retains under base capital or revolving capital plans, patronage refunds, and other

---

[*] In May 2003, the FASB issued FASB Statement of Financial Accounting Standards No. 150, *Accounting for Certain Financial Instruments With Characteristics of Both Liabilities and Equity.* This Statement establishes standards for how an issuer classifies and measures certain financial instruments with characteristics of both liabilities and equity. It requires that an issuer classify a financial instrument that is within its scope as a liability (or an asset in some circumstances). Many of those instruments were previously classified as equity.

This Standard may have a significant impact on financial statements of agricultural cooperatives. Retained allocated equities, including retains, which are usually repaid to cooperative patrons over a specific number of years generally meet the definition of mandatorily redeemable financial instruments under FASB Statement No. 150 and as such may have to be reclassified as liabilities. As a result, some agricultural cooperatives may report significantly reduced equities and increased liabilities in their GAAP financial statements.

In November 2003, the FASB issued FASB Staff Position (FSP) FAS 150-3, which defers the effective date of the mandatorily redeemable provisions of FASB Statement No. 150 and all related FSPs for nonpublic entities as follows: (*a*) until fiscal periods beginning after December 15, 2004 for instruments that are mandatorily redeemable on fixed dates and (*b*) indefinitely, pending further FASB action, if the redemption date is not fixed or if the payout amount is variable and not based on an index. Readers should be alert to further developments.

allocated equities. An investor cooperative may also be required to invest in some form of interest-bearing debt instrument.

11.12 To borrow from regional banks for cooperatives, investments in such banks are required. The extent of the investment is usually based on the amount and terms of the loans. Investments in the banks for cooperatives may also include capital stock received as patronage refunds.

Accounting Principles

11.13 Investments in other cooperatives should be accounted for at cost, including allocated equities and retains. For this purpose, cost means the amount of any cash investment and the face amount of all written notices of allocation in the form of per-unit retains, capital equity credits, revolving fund certificates, and certificates of equity.

11.14 The carrying amount of an investment in a cooperative should be reduced if the patron is unable to recover the full carrying value of the investment. Losses unallocated by the investee may indicate such an inability, and, at a minimum, the excess of unallocated losses over unallocated equities should be recognized by the patron, based on the patron's proportionate share of the total equity of the investee cooperative or any other appropriate method, unless the patron demonstrates a likelihood that the carrying amount of the investment in the cooperative can be fully recovered. Factors to consider in making the determination include—

- Whether the unallocated losses resulted from identifiable, isolated, and nonrecurring events.
- Whether the investee cooperative has been profitable over a long period of time and suffered only occasional losses that were offset by unallocated earnings or equities.
- Whether the investor has ceased or will cease to patronize the investee cooperative on a permanent basis or for an extended period of time.

11.15 Patrons should recognize patronage refunds either on notification by the distributing cooperative or when the related patronage occurs if it is then probable that (1) a patronage refund applicable to the period will be declared, (2) one or more future events confirming the receipt of a patronage refund are expected to occur, (3) the amount of the refund can be reasonably estimated, and (4) the accrual can be consistently made from year to year. The accrual should be based on the latest available reliable information and should be adjusted on notification of allocation.

11.16 Classification of the allocations in the financial statements should follow the recording of the costs or proceeds, or the allocations should be presented separately.

11.17 When a cooperative allocates all earnings to patrons (on a tax or book basis) and there are no unallocated earnings (on a book basis), the principles set forth in APB Opinion No. 18, *The Equity Method of Accounting for Investments in Common Stock,* are not applicable. In those infrequent instances where the investor's share of unallocated retained earnings of an investee cooperative is material to the investor, the equity method of accounting should be applied in a manner that gives consideration to the voting rules or statutory rights applicable to the cooperative.

11.18 Agricultural cooperatives should also consider guidance provided in FASB Interpretation No. 46 (revised December 2003), *Consolidation of Variable Interest Entities* (Interpretation No. 46R), when accounting for their investments in other cooperatives. See paragraphs 12.20 and 12.21 for a discussion of this Interpretation.

Auditing Considerations

11.19 SAS No. 92, *Auditing Derivative Instruments, Hedging Activities, and Investments in Securities* (AICPA, *Professional Standards,* vol. 1, AU sec. 332), provides guidance on auditing investments in debt and equity securities and investments accounted for under APB Opinion No. 18. Practitioners should refer to the auditing considerations and requirements of SAS No. 92, as applicable, for the guidance. In addition, the companion Audit Guide *Auditing Derivative Instruments, Hedging Activities, and Investments in Securities,* provides practical guidance for implementing SAS No. 92. For investments in cooperatives the auditor should analyze the investment accounts for the period and examine the documentation supporting the transactions, including securities on hand.

11.20 An investor will normally receive notification of amounts allocated by the investee cooperative, and the auditor should consider direct confirmation with the investee cooperative. If patronage refunds are accrued before notices of allocation have been received, the accrual should be tested for reasonableness and consistency. Consideration should be given to reviewing the estimated amount with the investee cooperatives.

11.21 The auditor should review the issuer's accounting for qualified and nonqualified allocations. It should be determined that these allocations were made in proper form and within the prescribed time limit.

11.22 In evaluating the carrying amounts of investments in other cooperatives, the auditor should consider the investor's continued participation in the investee cooperative and recent reliable financial information about the investee. Where the carrying amounts are material to the financial position of the investor cooperative and possible disclosure may be necessary, a more detailed review of the operations and financial status of the investee cooperative should be considered. If the carrying amount of an investment has been or should be reduced, the auditor should review financial information and obtain support showing that the investor cooperative will be unable to fully recover the carrying amount of the investment.

Equities and Members' Investments[*]

Background and Unique Characteristics

11.23 The composition of the equity section of a cooperative's balance sheet distinguishes it from other balance sheets. Generally, its equities arise

---

[*] In May 2003, the FASB issued FASB Statement of Financial Accounting Standards No. 150, *Accounting for Certain Financial Instruments With Characteristics of Both Liabilities and Equity.* This Statement establishes standards for how an issuer classifies and measures certain financial instruments with characteristics of both liabilities and equity. It requires that an issuer classify a financial instrument that is within its scope as a liability (or an asset in some circumstances). Many of those instruments were previously classified as equity.

This Standard may have a significant impact on financial statements of agricultural cooperatives. Retained allocated equities, including retains, which are usually repaid to cooperative patrons over a specific number of years generally meet the definition of mandatorily redeemable financial instruments under FASB Statement No. 150 and as such may have to be reclassified as liabilities. As a result, some agricultural cooperatives may report significantly reduced equities and increased liabilities in their GAAP financial statements.

In November 2003, the FASB issued FASB Staff Position (FSP) FAS 150-3, which defers the effective date of the mandatorily redeemable provisions of FASB Statement No. 150 and all related FSPs for nonpublic entities as follows: (*a*) until fiscal periods beginning after December 15, 2004 for instruments that are mandatorily redeemable on fixed dates and (*b*) indefinitely, pending further FASB action, if the redemption date is not fixed or if the payout amount is variable and not based on an index. Readers should be alert to further developments.

from investments by members and nonmembers and from patronage allocations. In addition, cooperatives may accumulate unallocated retained earnings arising from after-tax earnings on nonpatronage business.

Accounting Principles

11.24 Various forms of allocated equities arising from patronage are used by cooperatives. A brief description of those commonly used follows.

1. *Retained patronage allocations.* Retaining patronage earnings through methods such as the issuance of qualified or nonqualified written notices of allocation is a major form of financing by cooperatives.

2. *Per-unit retains.* Per-unit retains are used in marketing cooperatives in accordance with debt agreements, bylaws, or board of directors' authorizations. These amounts are determined without regard to earnings and may be based on a rate per ton or on a percentage of the dollar amount of raw product delivered. Amounts are withheld from payments to patrons for deliveries of raw products and are credited to the account of each patron.

11.25 If the retained patronage allocations and per-unit retains have no fixed maturity dates and are subordinated to all debt instruments, they should be treated as equity with appropriate disclosure of face value, dividend rate, negotiability, subordination agreements, and any revolving or retirement plan.

11.26 Allocated equities are usually paid, or revolved, over a number of years. The timing may be specified in the cooperative's bylaws, but it is usually at the discretion of its board of directors. The amounts should not be classified as current liabilities until the board has formally acted to revolve the equities.

11.27 In addition to allocated equities, cooperatives may issue common and preferred stock. Common stock is often issued to establish members' voting rights, whereas preferred stock may be sold to members and nonmembers on a nonpatronage basis. Cooperatives may also issue preferred stock as a form of earnings distribution. Limited amounts of dividends on preferred stock are tax deductible by exempt cooperatives, but they are not tax deductible by nonexempt cooperatives. Disclosure of a cooperative's equity is similar to that required for other corporate entities.

11.28 Certain transactions of cooperatives may result in unallocated equities. For example, cooperatives may derive earnings from nonpatronage business and account for these earnings as other corporations do. Nonpatronage earnings are frequently not allocated and are classified as retained earnings in the equity section. In addition, a cooperative may elect at times not to allocate patronage earnings or losses.

Auditing Considerations

11.29 The following procedures should be considered when auditing a cooperative's equity account.

1. Procedures for patronage allocations and per-unit retains are—
   - Becoming familiar with bylaws, board policies, and other governance documents regarding revolvement practices.
   - Examining, on a test basis, individual records of patrons' equity and test allocations and revolvements for compliance with bylaws and board minutes.
   - Considering whether allocation and revolvement provisions comply with statutory requirements.

- Confirming balances in various equity classifications with patrons.
- Reviewing allocations that are due to be retired within a year, and considering whether they should be reclassified as liabilities.
- Ascertaining that unallocated equities are indeed unallocated and that there are no special provisions or restrictions that should be disclosed.

2. Procedures for common and preferred stock are—
  - Considering compliance with statutory requirements, bylaw provisions, and articles of incorporation.
  - Reviewing minutes of the meetings of members and of the board of directors for approval of changes in capital structure.
  - Reviewing provisions of stock issuance for possible redemption requirements and the need for reclassification as a liability.

Current and Deferred Income Taxes

Background and Unique Characteristics

11.30 The various exemptions and deductions available to cooperatives have been discussed in prior sections of this guide. The applicable federal income tax provisions are found in sections 521 and 1381 through 1388 of the Internal Revenue Code. State income tax laws may also have applicable provisions.

11.31 Accounting for current and deferred income taxes of cooperatives is affected by several factors. These include whether patronage allocations are issued on a qualified or nonqualified basis, whether patronage allocations are based on book earnings or tax earnings, the classification of earnings as patronage or nonpatronage, and the status of the cooperatives as exempt or nonexempt.

11.32 Cooperatives may issue patronage allocations on a qualified or nonqualified basis. Generally, patronage distributions are considered qualified when at least 20 percent of the distribution is paid in cash and the balance distributed as qualified written notices of allocation within the required time period. Qualified patronage allocations are deductible for federal income tax purposes in the year for which they are issued and are fully taxable to the patrons in the year received. When cooperatives issue nonqualified notices of allocation, they are not currently deductible for federal income tax purposes, and the patrons do not recognize taxable income until payment is received.

11.33 Because of the tax treatment afforded tax-exempt cooperatives, accounting records should provide the patronage information necessary to determine that the cooperative has maintained its tax-exempt status. If the cooperative is nonexempt, the accounting records should identify patronage and nonpatronage income to facilitate the determination of patronage allocations and taxable income. Records should be maintained to provide information for determination of the costs associated with patronage and nonpatronage income.

11.34 The manner in which a patronage allocation is made is usually specified in the bylaws, resolutions of the board of directors, and marketing or other agreements. Whether allocations are based on book or tax earnings is usually controlled by bylaw provisions or action of the board of directors. Thus, both exempt and nonexempt cooperatives may have temporary differences as a result of differences in the accounting treatment of deductions and patronage allocations for financial and tax-reporting purposes.

Accounting Principles

11.35 As stated above, cooperatives are subject to income taxes as required under the reference sections of the Internal Revenue Code. When temporary differences exist, taxable income at the cooperative level may give rise to deferred taxes.

11.36 Generally, deferred tax accounting is not required for tax-temporary differences associated with patronage and nonpatronage earnings of exempt cooperatives and patronage earnings of nonexempt cooperatives when those earnings are allocated to patrons through use of qualified notices of allocation. In those circumstances, the liability for income taxes, current and deferred, follows the allocation of earnings and is the responsibility of the recipient patron.

11.37 For temporary differences related to nonqualified written notices of allocation of exempt and nonexempt cooperatives, nonpatronage earnings of nonexempt cooperatives, and patronage earnings not allocated as patronage refunds, FASB Statement No. 109 applies.

11.38 Accounting for deferred income taxes of a cooperative is affected by several factors. One such factor is whether or not patronage is allocated on a book or tax basis; other factors include the impact of patronage versus nonpatronage earnings and the use of nonqualified written notices of allocation.

Auditing Considerations

11.39 When reviewing a cooperative's tax liability, the auditor should consider—

1. Reviewing marketing and other contracts between the cooperative and its patrons and nonpatrons.
2. Reviewing the bylaws and articles of incorporation for their effect on patronage deductions.
3. Determining that a bylaw consent effective under Internal Revenue Code section 1388(c) or (h) has been adopted and that notice has been given to new members. (If no bylaw consent is in effect, individual written consents from patrons or qualified checks issued in accordance with tax regulations should be reviewed.)
4. Reviewing the accounting methods used by the cooperative to determine earnings subject to patronage distributions.
5. Reviewing the minutes approving the per-unit retain and annual patronage distribution to members.
6. Determining that allocations of patronage distributions and per-unit retains are made pursuant to written obligations in effect prior to the delivery of agricultural products or purchases of goods and services by patrons (see Internal Revenue Code section 1388).
7. Determining that patronage distributions, per-unit retains, and payments in cash claimed as deductions for the previous year were paid or issued with proper notice to patrons during the eight-and-one-half-month period after year-end.
8. Inquiring whether an exempt cooperative has engaged in activities that could result in the loss of its exempt status.
9. Determining that appropriate records are maintained for each patronage allocation unit and that separate earnings allocations are made on the basis of business transacted within each allocation unit.

PART III — Other Matters

Chapter 12

Other Accounting Principles and Auditing Considerations Applicable to Agricultural Producers and Agricultural Cooperatives*

Use of Derivative Instruments and Hedging Activities
Background

> The following section provides a discussion about the economic uses of derivative instruments and hedging activities. For accounting guidance on those topics the practitioner should refer to FASB Statement No. 133, as amended.

12.01 Forward contracts can be used to reduce the risk of loss from price fluctuations of products to be sold or materials to be purchased.

12.02 Both agricultural producers and agricultural cooperatives enter into marketing agreements with buyers, merchandisers, processors, and suppliers to assure a sales market or source of goods at a specific or determinable price. These agreements, called *forward contracts*, usually relate to the delivery of a fixed quantity of product or the delivery of all the product of a designated number of acres. These agreements usually also lock in a delivery date or period for delivery. Terms of the contracts vary by product type and the geographical area of the country.

12.03 A fixed-quantity contract requires the delivery of a fixed quantity of the specified product by a particular date. The price may be fixed at the time the contract is executed, established at the date of delivery, or established at a later date by basing it on a defined relationship to a quoted market price. The contract may provide for deferred payment of all or part of the contract amount.

12.04 An acreage contract requires the delivery of all the crop produced on a specified number of acres. The price may be fixed on a per-unit basis or may vary with quoted market prices in the same manner as fixed-quantity contracts and may be similarly deferred. Payment may be deferred as well.

12.05 Forward contracts may provide protection against the risk of loss from price variations that can result from the impact of the many factors that influence the supply and demand for agricultural products and supplies. However, forward contracts do not provide protection to the producer or cooperative if it is unable to meet its delivery obligation under the contract or if a supplier fails to perform in accordance with its commitment.

12.06 Trading in futures contracts for agricultural commodities has been possible through long established commodity exchanges. In recent years, the options markets have provided an alternative to the futures market for hedging transactions.

---

* Auditors of issuers need to refer to the Preface of this Guide for important information related to the PCAOB.

12.07 A producer or cooperative holding grain in inventory might hedge the risk of loss by selling futures contracts for an equivalent quantity of the same grain on a commodity futures market for delivery in the desired month of sale. Hedging with futures contracts reduces the risk of loss from unfavorable price changes and also effectively eliminates the possibility of gain from later favorable price changes.

12.08 As an alternative to the futures contract, the holder of the grain might purchase a put option covering an equivalent quantity of grain that would give the holder of the put the right to sell the grain to the writer of the put at the strike price and during the time specified in the contract. If the grain price had fallen by the exercise date, the put would be exercised at the higher strike price. If the grain price had risen by an amount greater than the contracted strike price, the put holder could benefit by allowing the option to expire and selling the grain at the higher market price.

12.09 A producer or cooperative may wish protection against a prospective increase in the cost of materials or supplies. This protection may be provided by purchasing futures contracts for the quantities expected to be needed at the contract delivery dates. For example, a producer with large numbers of animals to feed might buy grain futures contracts in amounts and for delivery dates that coincide with projected needs.

12.10 As an alternative, the producer might acquire a call option giving the holder the right to purchase the specified quantity of grain at the contract strike price during an option term that includes the date on which the grain was expected to be needed. If the price of the grain on the market had fallen below the strike price by more than the cost of the call, the holder could allow the call option to expire and benefit by purchasing the grain at the lower current market price. If the market price had risen, the right to purchase the grain at the lower strike price would be exercised.

12.11 In economic (not accounting) terms, hedges are classified as either buying (long) hedges or selling (short) hedges. Buying hedges may be used, for example, to fix the cost or assure the availability of a commodity when producers or cooperatives have entered into fixed-price sales commitments or to fix the purchase price of commodities to be used in production or processing. Examples of uses of selling hedges would be to establish sales prices when producers or cooperatives hold inventory for sale or to provide protection when fixed-price purchase commitments have been made.

12.12 Not all commodities that producers and cooperatives may wish to hedge are traded on futures exchanges. However, a substitute commodity that is traded on a futures exchange may be used to establish an economic hedge if there is a clear economic relationship between the prices of the two commodities and high correlation is probable. Those transactions are referred to as *cross hedges*.

12.13 A producer may establish an economic hedge position for the future sale of a crop before it is harvested and, at times, before it is planted.

12.14 Usually, deliveries are not made against futures contracts. Rather, the contracts are closed by buying or selling an offsetting number of contracts on the futures exchange when the underlying commodity is purchased or sold.

12.15 Some agricultural cooperatives also use interest-rate swaps to hedge the uncertain future cash flows associated with variable-rate debt.

Accounting for Derivative Instruments and Hedging Activities

12.16 FASB Statement No. 133, *Accounting for Derivative Instruments and Hedging Activities*, as amended by FASB Statements No. 137, *Accounting for Derivative Instruments and Hedging Activities—Deferral of the Effective*

Date, No. 138, *Accounting for Certain Derivative Instruments and Certain Hedging Activities, an Amendment of FASB Statement No. 133*, and No. 149, *Amendment of Statement 133 on Derivative Instruments and Hedging Activities*, establishes accounting and reporting standards for derivative instruments, including certain derivative instruments embedded in other contracts (collectively referred to as derivatives), and for hedging activities. It requires that an entity recognize all derivatives as either assets or liabilities in the statement of financial position and measure those instruments at fair value. If certain conditions are met, a derivative may be specifically designated as (*a*) a hedge of the exposure to changes in the fair value of a recognized asset or liability or an unrecognized firm commitment, (*b*) a hedge of the exposure to variable cash flows of a forecasted transaction, or (*c*) a hedge of the foreign currency exposure of a net investment in a foreign operation, an unrecognized firm commitment, an available-for-sale security, or a foreign-currency-denominated forecasted transaction. The accounting for changes in the fair value of a derivative (that is, gains and losses) depends on the intended use of the derivative and the resulting designation. Certain forward contracts that otherwise meet the definition of derivatives are excluded from the scope of FASB Statement No. 133 under the "normal purchases and normal sales" provision as described in paragraph 10(b) of that Statement. Paragraphs 44 through 47 of FASB Statement No. 133, as amended, contains extensive disclosure requirements. Readers should refer to the full text of the Statement and related amendments when considering accounting and reporting issues related to derivative instruments and hedging activities. The FASB established the Derivatives Implementation Group (DIG) to assist the Board and its staff in providing implementation guidance regarding FASB Statement No. 133. Issues addressed by the DIG and the status of related guidance can be found at the FASB's Web site at www.fasb.org.

Auditing Considerations

12.17 Audit procedures should be designed to determine the existence and proper reporting of marketing agreements and should include—

1. Obtaining an understanding of normal purchasing and marketing methods.

2. Inquiring and obtaining written representations[1] from management and owners.

3. Reviewing transactions subsequent to the balance sheet date for undisclosed agreements.

4. Reviewing open contracts and confirming details with other parties.

5. Obtaining and evaluating the facts required for making a judgment about (*a*) the need to decrease the carrying amount of existing inventories or (*b*) the need to recognize a loss resulting from open marketing agreements.

12.18 SAS No. 92, *Auditing Derivative Instruments, Hedging Activities, and Investments in Securities* (AICPA, *Professional Standards*, vol. 1, AU sec. 332), provides guidance on auditing investments in debt and equity securities, investments accounted for under APB Opinion No. 18, and derivative instru-

---

[1] SAS No. 85, *Management Representations*, as amended by SAS No. 89, *Audit Adjustments*, and SAS No. 99, *Consideration of Fraud in a Financial Statement Audit* (AICPA, *Professional Standards*, vol. 1, AU sec. 333), establishes a requirement that an auditor, performing an audit in accordance with generally accepted auditing standards, obtain written representations for all financial statements and periods covered by the auditor's report. The Statement also provides guidance concerning the representations to be obtained, along with an illustrative management representation letter.

ments and hedging activities. Practitioners should also be aware about the existence of a companion Audit Guide to SAS No. 92 entitled *Auditing Derivative Instruments, Hedging Activities, and Investments in Securities*. The purpose of the guide is to provide practical guidance for implementing the SAS on all types of audit engagements. The suggested auditing procedures contained in the guide do not increase or otherwise modify the auditor's responsibilities described in SAS No. 92. Rather, the suggested procedures in the guide are intended to clarify and illustrate the application of the requirements of SAS No. 92. Practitioners should refer to the auditing considerations and requirements of SAS No. 92 and the guidance contained in the related Audit Guide.

Asset Retirement Obligations

12.19 With rapid change in production technology, asset retirement obligations have become a significant consideration for agricultural producers and cooperatives. FASB Statement No. 143, *Accounting for Asset Retirement Obligations*, addresses financial accounting and reporting for obligations associated with the retirement of tangible long-lived assets and the associated asset retirement costs. It applies to legal obligations associated with the retirement of long-lived assets that result from the acquisition, construction, development and (or) the normal operation of a long-lived asset, except for certain obligations of lessees. As used in FASB Statement No. 143, a legal obligation is an obligation that a party is required to settle as a result of an existing or enacted law, statute, ordinance, or written or oral contract or by legal construction of a contract under the doctrine of a promissory estoppel. FASB Statement No. 143 requires that the fair value of a liability for an asset retirement obligation be recognized in the period in which it is incurred if a reasonable estimate of fair value can be made. If a reasonable estimate of fair value cannot be made in the period the asset retirement obligation is incurred, the liability shall be recognized when a reasonable estimate of fair value can be made. Upon initial recognition of a liability for an asset retirement obligation, an entity shall capitalize an asset retirement cost by increasing the carrying amount of the related long-lived asset by the same amount as the liability. An entity shall subsequently allocate that asset retirement cost to expense using a systematic and rational method over its useful life.[2]

Consolidation of Variable Interest Entities

12.20 Agricultural producers and cooperatives should consider guidance provided in FASB Interpretation No. 46 (revised December 2003), *Consolidation of Variable Interest Entities* (Interpretation No. 46R),[*] when accounting for

---

[2] SAS No. 101, *Auditing Fair Value Measurements and Disclosures*, contains significantly expanded guidance on the audit procedures for fair value measurements and disclosures contained in financial statements. Please refer to paragraphs 12.40–12.43 for more information on SAS No. 101.

[*] FASB Interpretation No. 46R was issued in December 2003 and replaces FASB Interpretation No. 46, *Consolidation of Variable Interest Entities* (Interpretation No. 46), which was issued in January 2003. Special effective date provisions of Interpretation No. 46R apply to enterprises that have fully or partially applied Interpretation No. 46 prior to issuance of this revised Interpretation. Otherwise, application of Interpretation No. 46R (or Interpretation No. 46) is required in financial statements of public entities that have interests in structures that are commonly referred to as special-purpose entities for periods ending after December 15, 2003. Application by public entities, other than small business issuers, for all other types of variable interest entities is required in financial statements for periods ending after March 15, 2004. Application by small business issuers to variable interest entities other than special-purpose entities and by nonpublic entities to all types of variable interest entities is required at various dates in 2004 and 2005. In some instances, enterprises have the option of applying or continuing to apply Interpretation No. 46 for a short period of time before applying this revised Interpretation. Please refer to Interpretation No. 46R for more information.

their investments in agricultural cooperatives and other entities. Agricultural producers involved in cash or crop-sharing agreements[3] whereby the landowner controls both the producer and the entity operating the land, may also be subject to provisions of FASB Interpretation No. 46R. Interpretation No. 46R addresses consolidation by business enterprises of entities to which the usual condition of consolidation described in Accounting Research Bulletin (ARB) No. 51, *Consolidated Financial Statements*, does not apply, either because the equity investors in an entity (*a*) do not have the characteristics of a controlling financial interest, or (*b*) do not have sufficient equity at risk for the entity to finance its activities without additional subordinated financial support. An entity lacking one of these characteristics is referred to as a variable interest entity (VIE). Interpretation No. 46R governs how entities should assess interests in other entities in determining whether to consolidate (or deconsolidate) that entity. Interpretation No. 46R requires an assessment of every relationship between an enterprise and another legal entity. Legal entities include grantor trusts, limited liability corporations, partnerships, corporations, and other trusts. Broadly stated, an entity that must determine consolidation in accordance with Interpretation No. 46R is known as a VIE and an entity that is required to consolidate a VIE is known as a primary beneficiary. There are many possible relationships an enterprise may have with other legal entities that are VIEs. For example, a company may participate in joint ventures with outside investors that may be VIEs. Swap agreements and derivative instruments between entities, even if used for hedging purposes, need to be evaluated. Management needs to evaluate equity method investments, leases, trust accounts, and loans as potential relationships with a VIE that may trigger consolidation.

12.21 Interpretation No. 46R changes prior practices by requiring a company to consolidate a VIE if that company either is subject to a majority of the risk of loss from the VIE's activities or is entitled to receive a majority of the VIE's residual returns, or both.

Audit Documentation[*]

12.22 The auditor should prepare and maintain audit documentation, the form and content of which should be designed to meet the circumstances of the

---

[3] See paragraph 2.03 for more information on these arrangements.

[*] The PCAOB has issued (1) a proposed auditing standard, *Audit Documentation*, and an amendment to their Interim Auditing Standards, and (2) Auditing Standard No. 2, *An Audit of Internal Control Over Financial Reporting Performed in Conjunction With an Audit of Financial Statements*. At the time of development of this edition of the Guide, these standards were not yet approved by the SEC and were therefore not effective. If approved by the SEC, these standards would apply to audits of financial statements of issuers, as defined by the Sarbanes-Oxley Act, and other entities when prescribed by the rules of the SEC (collectively referred to as "issuers").

The proposed *Audit Documentation* Standard would supersede AU sec. 339 of the PCAOB's Interim Standards. The proposed Standard would establish general requirements for documentation the auditor should prepare and retain in connection with any engagement conducted in accordance with Auditing and related Professional Practice Standards of the PCAOB.

PCAOB Auditing Standard No. 2 establishes requirements that apply when an auditor is engaged to audit both an issuer's financial statements and management's assessment of the effectiveness of internal control over financial reporting. PCAOB Auditing Standard No. 2 provides that in addition to the documentation requirements contained in AU sec. 339 of the PCAOB's Interim Standards, the auditor should document certain items related to their audit of internal control over financial reporting.

See the Preface of this Guide for more detailed information. Registered public accounting firms must comply with the Standards of the PCAOB in connection with the preparation or issuance of any audit report on the financial statements of an issuer and in their auditing and related attestation practices. Registered public accounting firms auditing the financial statements of issuers should keep alert to the final status of these PCAOB standards.

particular audit engagement. Audit documentation is the principal record of auditing procedures applied, evidence obtained, and conclusions reached by the auditor in the engagement. The quantity, type, and content of audit documentation are matters of the auditor's professional judgment.

12.23 Audit documentation serves mainly to:

a.   Provide the principal support for the auditor's report, including the representation regarding observance of the standards of fieldwork, which is implicit in the reference in the report to generally accepted auditing standards.[4]

b.   Aid the auditor in the conduct and supervision of the audit.

12.24 Examples of audit documentation are audit programs,[5] analyses, memoranda, letters of confirmation and representation, abstracts or copies of entity documents, and schedules or commentaries prepared or obtained by the auditor. Audit documentation may be in paper form, electronic form, or other media.

12.25 Audit documentation should be sufficient to (a) enable members of the engagement team with supervision and review responsibilities to understand the nature, timing, extent, and results of auditing procedures performed, and the evidence obtained;[6] (b) indicate the engagement team member(s) who performed and reviewed the work; and (c) show that the accounting records agree or reconcile with the financial statements or other information being reported on.

12.26 In addition to the requirements discussed in paragraphs 12.22– 12.25 above, SAS No. 96, *Audit Documentation* (AICPA, *Professional Standards*, vol. 1, AU sec. 339), provides further requirements about the content, ownership and confidentiality of audit documentation. Moreover, Appendix A to SAS No. 96 lists the audit documentation requirements contained in other statements on auditing standards.

12.27 Effective for audits and reviews completed on or after October 31, 2003, the SEC rule *Retention of Records Relevant to Audits and Reviews* requires accounting firms to retain for seven years certain records relevant to their audits and reviews of issuers' financial statements. These records include workpapers and other documents that form the basis of the audit or review, and memoranda, correspondence, communications, other documents, and records (including electronic records), which are created, sent or received in connection with the audit or review, and contain conclusions, opinions, analyses, or financial data related to the audit or review. See SEC Release No. 33-8180 for more information.

---

[4] However, there is no intention to imply that the auditor would be precluded from supporting his or her report by other means in addition to audit documentation.

[5] See Statement on Auditing Standards (SAS) No. 22, *Planning and Supervision* (AICPA, *Professional Standards*, vol. 1, AU sec. 311.05), for guidance regarding preparation of audit programs.

[6] A firm of independent auditors has a responsibility to adopt a system of quality control policies and procedures to provide the firm with reasonable assurance that its personnel comply with applicable professional standards, including generally accepted auditing standards, and the firm's standards of quality in conducting individual audit engagements. Review of audit documentation and discussions with engagement team members are among the procedures a firm performs when monitoring compliance with the quality control policies and procedures that it has established. (Also, see SAS No. 25, *The Relationship of Generally Accepted Auditing Standards to Quality Control Standards* [AICPA, *Professional Standards*, vol. 1, AU sec. 161].)

The Auditor's Consideration of Internal Control in a Financial Statement Audit[*]

Background

12.28 *Agricultural Producers.* Internal control that is appropriate for agricultural producers is similar to that appropriate for entities engaged in manufacturing. Controls normally exist over the producer's major transaction cycles, such as purchasing, sales, and payroll. In addition, the producer normally maintains controls over production activities that provide reasonable assurance that costs are appropriately allocated to inventories and self-constructed assets.

12.29 *Agricultural Cooperatives.* Agricultural cooperatives usually establish controls that are similar to those of other commercial enterprises. Controls normally exist over the cooperative's major transaction cycles, such as marketing, purchasing, production, and payroll. Also, internal control usually provides reasonable assurance that transactions and activities undertaken by the cooperative are understood and authorized by the board of directors.

Authoritative Guidance

12.30 SAS No. 55, *Consideration of Internal Control in a Financial Statement Audit*, as amended by SAS No. 78, *Consideration of Internal Control in a Financial Statement Audit: An Amendment to SAS No. 55*, and by SAS No. 94, *The Effect of Information Technology on the Auditor's Consideration of Internal Control in a Financial Statement Audit*, defines internal control, describes the objectives and components of internal control, and explains how an auditor should consider internal control in planning and performing an audit. In all audits, the auditor should obtain an understanding of internal control sufficient to plan the audit by performing procedures to understand the design of controls relevant to an audit of financial statements and determining whether they have been placed in operation. In obtaining this understanding, the auditor considers how an entity's use of information technology (IT)[7] and manual procedures may affect controls relevant to the audit. The auditor then assesses control risk for the assertions embodied in the account balance, transaction class, and disclosure components of the financial statements.

---

[*] In March 2004, the PCAOB issued Auditing Standard No. 2, *An Audit of Internal Control Over Financial Reporting Performed in Conjunction With an Audit of Financial Statements*. At the time of development of this edition of the Guide, this Standard was not approved by the SEC and was therefore not effective. If approved by the SEC, this Standard would apply to audits of the financial statements of issuers, as defined by the Sarbanes-Oxley Act, and other entities when prescribed by the rules of the SEC (collectively referred to as "issuers"). PCAOB Auditing Standard No. 2 establishes requirements that apply when an auditor is engaged to audit both an issuer's financial statements and management's assessment of the effectiveness of internal control over financial reporting. Due to the issuance of PCAOB Auditing Standard No. 2, a related proposed Standard (PCAOB Release No. 2004-002) would amend and supersede certain sections of the PCAOB interim standards. See the Preface of this Guide for more detailed information. Registered public accounting firms must comply with the Standards of the PCAOB in connection with the preparation or issuance of any audit report on the financial statements of an issuer and in their auditing and related attestation practices. Registered public accounting firms auditing the financial statements of issuers should keep alert to final SEC approval of this PCAOB Standard.

[7] Information technology (IT) encompasses automated means of originating, processing, storing, and communicating information, and includes recording devices, communication systems, computer systems (including hardware and software components and data), and other electronic devices. An entity's use of IT may be extensive; however, the auditor is primarily interested in the entity's use of IT to initiate, record, process, and report transactions or other financial data.

12.31 The auditor may determine that assessing control risk below the maximum level[8] for certain assertions would be effective and more efficient than performing only substantive tests. In addition, the auditor may determine that it is not practical or possible to restrict detection risk to an acceptable level by performing only substantive tests for one or more financial statement assertions. In such circumstances, the auditor should obtain evidential matter about the effectiveness of both the design and operation of controls to reduce the assessed level of control risk. Such evidential matter may be obtained from tests of controls planned and performed concurrent with or subsequent to obtaining the understanding.[9] Such evidential matter also may be obtained from procedures that were not specifically planned as tests of controls but that nevertheless provide evidential matter about the effectiveness of the design and operation of the controls. For certain assertions, the auditor may desire to further reduce the assessed level of control risk. In such cases, the auditor considers whether evidential matter sufficient to support a further reduction is likely to be available and whether performing additional tests of controls to obtain such evidential matter would be efficient.

12.32 Alternatively, the auditor may assess control risk at the maximum level because he or she believes controls are unlikely to pertain to an assertion or are unlikely to be effective, or because evaluating the effectiveness of controls would be inefficient. However, the auditor needs to be satisfied that performing only substantive tests would be effective in restricting detection risk to an acceptable level. When evidence of an entity's initiation, recording, or processing of financial data exists only in electronic form, the auditor's ability to obtain the desired assurance only from substantive tests would significantly diminish.

12.33 The auditor uses the understanding of internal control and the assessed level of control risk in determining the nature, timing, and extent of substantive tests for financial statement assertions.

Tests of Controls[*]

12.34 Procedures directed toward evaluating the effectiveness of the design of a control are concerned with whether that control is suitably designed to prevent or detect material misstatements in specific financial statement assertions. Procedures to obtain such evidential matter ordinarily include inquiries of appropriate entity personnel; inspection of documents, reports, or electronic files; and observation of the application of specific controls. For entities with complex internal control, the auditor should consider the use of flowcharts, questionnaires, or decision tables to facilitate the application of procedures directed toward evaluating the effectiveness of the design of a control.

12.35 Procedures to obtain evidential matter about the effectiveness of the operation of a control are referred to as tests of controls (paragraphs 90

---

[8] Control risk may be assessed in quantitative terms, such as percentages, or in nonquantitative terms that range, for example, from a maximum to a minimum. The term maximum level is used in SAS No. 55, as amended, to mean the greatest probability that a material misstatement that could occur in a financial statement assertion will not be prevented or detected on a timely basis by an entity's internal control.

[9] If the auditor is unable to obtain such evidential matter, he or she should consider the guidance in SAS No. 31, *Evidential Matter* (AICPA, *Professional Standards*, vol. 1, AU sec. 326.14 and 326.25), as amended by SAS No. 80, *Amendment to Statement on Auditing Standards No. 31, Evidential Matter.*

[*] See footnote * to the "Auditor's Consideration of Internal Control in a Financial Statement Audit" section in this chapter.

through 104 of SAS No. 55, as amended, discuss characteristics of evidential matter to consider when performing tests of controls). Tests of controls directed toward the operating effectiveness of a control are concerned with how the control (whether manual or automated) was applied, the consistency with which it was applied during the audit period, and by whom it was applied. These tests ordinarily include procedures such as inquiries of appropriate entity personnel; inspection of documents, reports, or electronic files indicating performance of the control; observation of the application of the control; and reperformance of the application of the control by the auditor. In some circumstances, a specific procedure may address the effectiveness of both design and operation. However, a combination of procedures may be necessary to evaluate the effectiveness of the design or operation of a control.

12.36 In designing tests of automated controls, the auditor should consider the need to obtain evidence supporting the effective operation of controls directly related to the assertions as well as other indirect controls on which these controls depend.

12.37 Because of the inherent consistency of IT processing, the auditor may be able to reduce the extent of testing of an automated control. For example, a programmed application control should function consistently unless the program (including the tables, files, or other permanent data used by the program) is changed. Once the auditor determines that an automated control is functioning as intended (which could be done at the time the control is initially implemented or at some other date), the auditor should consider performing tests to determine that the control continues to function effectively. Such tests might include determining that changes to the program are not made without being subject to the appropriate program change controls, that the authorized version of the program is used for processing transactions, and that other relevant general controls are effective. Such tests also might include determining that changes to the programs have not been made, as may be the case when the entity uses packaged software applications without modifying or maintaining them.

12.38 To test automated controls, the auditor may need to use techniques that are different from those used to test manual controls. For example, computer-assisted audit techniques may be used to test automated controls or data related to assertions. Also, the auditor may use other automated tools or reports produced by IT to test the operating effectiveness of general controls, such as program change controls, access controls, and system software controls. The auditor should consider whether specialized skills are needed to design and perform such tests of controls.

12.39 The conclusion reached as a result of assessing control risk is referred to as the assessed level of control risk. In determining the evidential matter necessary to support an assessed level of control risk below the maximum level, the auditor should consider the characteristics of the evidential matter about control risk discussed in SAS No. 55, as amended, paragraphs 90 through 104. Generally, however, the lower the assessed level of control risk, the greater the assurance the evidential matter must provide that the controls relevant to an assertion are designed and operating effectively.

Auditing Fair Value Measurements and Disclosures

12.40 Financial statements of agricultural producers and cooperatives contain a number of significant fair value measurements and disclosures. For example, fair value of investments in non-publicly-traded entities, such as other cooperatives, joint ventures, limited liability companies, and family limited partnerships are common to both agricultural producers and cooperatives. In addition, as investment strategies increasingly include investing in more complex and higher-risk securities, the values of securities may not be readily available through market quotations. Such securities are often valued at amounts determined by the cooperatives and producers' management. Auditing the valuation of investments in non-publicly-traded entities and certain securities is an area that requires a high degree of judgment to ensure that the valuation procedures are reasonable and underlying support is appropriate. SAS No. 101, *Auditing Fair Value Measurements and Disclosures* (AICPA, *Professional Standards*, vol. 1, AU sec. 328), contains significantly expanded guidance on the audit procedures for fair value measurements and disclosures.

12.41 SAS No. 101 provides overall guidance on auditing fair value measurements and disclosures. It does not, however, provide guidance on auditing specific assets, liabilities, components of equity, transactions, or industry-specific practices. That guidance will be developed in the future or is available in:

- Other standards, such as SAS No. 92, *Auditing Derivative Instruments, Hedging Activities, and Investments in Securities* (AU sec. 332)
- Nonauthoritative publications, such as the recently released auditor's toolkit entitled *Auditing Fair Value Measurements and Disclosures: Allocations of the Purchase Price Under FASB Statement of Financial Accounting Standards No. 141*, Business Combinations, *and Tests of Impairment Under FASB Statements No. 142*, Goodwill and Other Intangible Assets, *and No. 144*, Accounting for the Impairment or Disposal of Long-Lived Assets

12.42 Under SAS No. 101, the auditor's substantive tests of fair value measurements involve (*a*) testing management's significant assumptions, the valuation model, and the underlying data, (*b*) developing independent fair value estimates for corroborative purposes, or (*c*) examining subsequent events and transactions that confirm or disconfirm the estimate.

12.43 When testing management's significant assumptions, the valuation model, and the underlying data, the auditor evaluates whether:

1. Management's assumptions are reasonable and reflect, or are not inconsistent with, market information.

2. The fair value measurement was determined using an appropriate model, if applicable.

3. Management used relevant information that was reasonably available at the time.

Auditors should note that this evaluation is required even if the fair value estimate is made by a valuation specialist.

Chapter 13

Consideration of Fraud in a Financial Statement Audit

13.01 SAS No. 99, *Consideration of Fraud in a Financial Statement Audit*, is the primary source of authoritative guidance about an auditor's responsibilities concerning the consideration of fraud in a financial statement audit. SAS No. 99 supersedes SAS No. 82, *Consideration of Fraud in a Financial Statement Audit* (AICPA, *Professional Standards*, vol. 1, AU sec. 316), and amends SAS No. 1, section 230, *Due Professional Care in the Performance of Work* (AICPA, *Professional Standards*, vol. 1, AU sec. 230). SAS No. 99 establishes standards and provides guidance to auditors in fulfilling their responsibility to plan and perform the audit to obtain reasonable assurance about whether the financial statements are free of material misstatement, whether caused by error or fraud as stated in SAS No. 1, section 110, *Responsibilities and Functions of the Independent Auditor* (AICPA, *Professional Standards*, vol. 1, AU sec. 110.02). (SAS No. 99 also amends SAS No. 85, *Management Representations*.)

13.02 There are two types of misstatements relevant to the auditor's consideration of fraud in a financial statement audit: misstatements arising from fraudulent financial reporting and misstatements arising from misappropriation of assets. Additionally, three conditions generally are present when fraud occurs. First, management or other employees have an *incentive* or are under *pressure*, which provides a reason to commit fraud. Second, circumstances exist—for example, the absence of controls, ineffective controls, or the ability of management to override controls—that provide an *opportunity* for a fraud to be perpetrated. Third, those involved are able to *rationalize* committing a fraudulent act.

The Importance of Exercising Professional Skepticism

13.03 Because of the characteristics of fraud, the auditor's exercise of professional skepticism is important when considering the risk of material misstatement due to fraud. Professional skepticism is an attitude that includes a questioning mind and a critical assessment of audit evidence. The auditor should conduct the engagement with a mindset that recognizes the possibility that a material misstatement due to fraud could be present, regardless of any past experience with the entity and regardless of the auditor's belief about management's honesty and integrity. Furthermore, professional skepticism requires an ongoing questioning of whether the information and evidence obtained suggests that a material misstatement due to fraud has occurred.

Discussion Among Engagement Personnel Regarding the Risks of Material Misstatement Due to Fraud

13.04 Members of the audit team should discuss the potential for material misstatement due to fraud in accordance with the requirements of paragraphs 14–18 of SAS No. 99. The discussion among the audit team members about the susceptibility of the entity's financial statements to material misstatement due to fraud should include a consideration of the known external and internal factors affecting the entity that might (a) create incentives/pressures for management and others to commit fraud, (b) provide the opportunity for fraud to be perpetrated, and (c) indicate a culture or environment that enables management to rationalize committing fraud. Communication among the audit team members about the risks of material misstatement due to fraud also should continue throughout the audit.

13.05 Most agricultural cooperatives and producers exhibit the classic small business attributes. For example, top management (CEO, general manager, etc.) tends to dominate the entity, increasing the likelihood of override of controls. Basic controls may be in place, but segregation of duties is often lacking. Internal audit function is rarely present. Most agricultural cooperatives and farming operations are not publicly owned, and therefore are not subject to SEC and the requirements of the Sarbanes-Oxley Act. Generally, there is no audit committee and the board of directors lacks financial expertise. Management often lacks an understanding or appreciation of accounting and financial reporting standards. Likewise, the accounting staff may lack sophistication and an understanding of current accounting developments. At the same time, agricultural cooperatives and producers are becoming engaged in more and more complex financial transactions, such as those involving derivatives and significant estimates. Producers are becoming more diversified, adding vertical integration to the business by additional processing of the commodity beyond the traditional harvest point. The expanding agricultural entrepreneur likely began farming a much smaller acreage with fewer crops. As operations expand the accounting and financial expertise often lags behind.

13.06 The agriculture industry operates on a yearly cycle due to distinct planting, growing and harvesting seasons. Both cooperatives and producers operate in this seasonal environment. A high demand exists for seasonal and temporary employees. Such employees are likely to be compensated less than full-time employees and less likely to receive the full complement of benefits enjoyed by full-time employees. Such employees are less likely to be committed to the cooperative and more likely to misappropriate assets.

Examples of Fraud Risk Factors

13.07 The following are examples of fraud risk factors that may be present in agricultural cooperatives and producers.

Part 1:   Fraudulent Financial Reporting

A. *Incentives/Pressures*

- Performance-based compensation incentives
- Pressures to provide returns to members of cooperatives or non-active family members of agricultural producers
- Pressure to keep cooperative members and lenders satisfied by reporting consistent financial results from year to year despite the inherent volatility of the agricultural industry. Competition, supply and demand factors, weather, government programs, etc. all result in uncertain and unpredictable sales volumes, crop yields, commodity prices and profitability levels
- Need to report favorable financial results to stave off pressures to merge
- Need to report adequate earnings to finance capital acquisitions (e.g., different types of handling and storage facilities required for the identity preservation needed to capture the premiums of specialty crops, expansion of business through additional vertically integrated processing)

- Need to report adequate earnings in order to obtain future financing
- Need to meet financial targets to obtain business licensure (warehouse, etc.)
- Rapid developments in technology (biotechnology, chemicals, genetically modified organisms, animal genetics, etc.) that make inventories obsolete
- Desire to cover up losses resulting from the rejection of genetically-modified crops by key markets
- Potential losses on unhedged or imperfectly hedged commodity market positions
- Global or local trends in the agricultural economy that could result in reduced profitability, such as high degree of competition, market saturation in a mature market, declining margins, weather patterns that harm yields or infringe on key planting or harvesting periods, etc. that threaten the viability of members (collectibility of receivables, future sales opportunities, etc.)
- Government programs may significantly alter farmer planting and marketing decisions, thereby resulting in reduced sales, reduced margins and financial statement volatility. Government subsidies are a major component of some operations. Some producers and cooperatives may engage in fraudulent activities to receive yet more subsidies. For example, they may attempt to collect government payments for non-planting while continuing to plant, grow and harvest a crop. Another possibility would be to change the amount of acres of a crop planted and reported to another crop due to change in pricing structure.

B. *Opportunities*

- Small business characteristics such as domineering management, inadequate segregation of duties, absence of internal audit and audit committee, etc.
- Complex marketing and hedging activities
- Complex and numerous deferred tax issues
- Significant related party transactions. In a cooperative, the members of the board of directors also are members and customers of the cooperative. Virtually all customers also are member/owners. Therefore, most revenue-generating transactions are conducted with related parties. It is presumed that these transactions are routine, bona fide arms-length business transactions. It is thus difficult to identify any related-party activity that actually deserves enhanced scrutiny. In the case of agricultural producers, transfer prices of commodities between producers and related processing entities may be manipulated to achieve desired results.
- Valuation of agricultural products is highly subjective and often requires specialized knowledge
- Valuation of non-publicly-traded investments are based on significant estimates that involve subjective judgments
- Preparation of financial statements of agricultural producers and cooperatives requires use of estimates in a number of key areas (see paragraph 13.29 for a list of significant estimates used in the industry)
- Grain marketing cooperatives usually also operate as public warehouses. Commodities handled by the warehouse (e.g., wheat or corn) are fungible and cannot be specifically identified or differentiated as to ownership. Commodities owned by the warehouse are commingled

in bulk storage with commodities owned by depositors. This results in the opportunity to overstate inventory and profitability by suppressing the storage obligation to depositors.

- Complex organizational structures involving joint ventures, subsidiaries, limited liability companies, etc.

C. Attitudes/Rationalizations

- Desire to report adequate earnings to justify a distribution to members
- Cover up bad decisions, poor management, etc.

Part 2: Misappropriation of Assets

A. Incentives/Pressures

- Employees uncertain about continued employment in light of financial stress on the cooperative
- Seasonal or temporary employees with less commitment to the cooperative, lower pay and absence of benefits
- Lower wage scale in relation to other industries

B. Opportunities

- Inventory items of small size with high value (e.g., agricultural chemicals)
- Inventories consisting of fungible commodities, easily convertible to cash
- Commingling of company-owned assets with assets owned by third-party depositors in a public warehouse
- Commingling of assets and/or liabilities within related party entities
- Agricultural supply businesses (equipment dealerships, fertilizer and chemical companies, etc.) frequently offer deferred billing arrangements to buyers of their products. Producers and cooperatives may use these arrangements to manipulate their financial results by not recognizing liability for such products in the proper period. If a cooperative sells products to its members under deferred billing arrangement, customer account statements are often not provided during the deferred billing periods. This makes it possible to obscure or distort accounts receivable aging problems, lapping schemes, etc.
- Inventory stored at remote, rural, poorly secured locations
- Numerous remote sites with few employees, inadequate segregation of duties, and inadequate supervision by top management
- Supplier rebate programs that are handled outside the routine accounting process and change from year to year
- Inherent conflicts of interest wherein employees with access to inventories also use those products in their own outside activities (e.g., farming or custom chemical and fertilizer application)

C. Attitudes/Rationalizations

- Unreasonable reliance on fundamental integrity of the agricultural community in general. Many members of the agricultural community consider it to be a close-knit community with a high level of moral and ethical standards. Therefore, inadequate attention may be paid to internal controls, written documentation of transactions and agreements, follow-up on unusual or unexpected items, etc.
- Small losses cost less than the cost of controls to prevent them.

Obtaining the Information Needed to Identify the Risks of Material Misstatement Due to Fraud

13.08 SAS No. 22, *Planning and Supervision* (AU sec. 311.06–.08), provides guidance about how the auditor obtains knowledge about the entity's business and the industry in which it operates. In performing that work, information may come to the auditor's attention that should be considered in identifying risks of material misstatement due to fraud. As part of this work, the auditor should perform the following procedures to obtain information that is used (as described in paragraphs 35 through 42 of SAS No. 99) to identify the risks of material misstatement due to fraud:

  a. Make inquiries of management and others within the entity to obtain their views about the risks of fraud and how they are addressed. (See paragraphs 20 through 27 of SAS No. 99.)

  b. Consider any unusual or unexpected relationships that have been identified in performing analytical procedures in planning the audit. (See paragraphs 28 through 30 of SAS No. 99.)

  c. Consider whether one or more fraud risk factors exist. (See paragraphs 31 through 33 of SAS No. 99, the Appendix to SAS No. 99 and paragraphs 13.07, 13.16, and 13.17.)

  d. Consider other information that may be helpful in the identification of risks of material misstatement due to fraud. (See paragraph 34 of SAS No. 99.)

13.09 In planning the audit, the auditor also should perform analytical procedures relating to revenue with the objective of identifying unusual or unexpected relationships involving revenue accounts that may indicate a material misstatement due to fraudulent financial reporting.

13.10 Developing expectations and evaluating the results of analytical procedures may be difficult because of the inherent volatility of many businesses in which agricultural cooperatives and producers are involved. For example, the timing and volume of crop input sales as well as production yields can vary greatly from one year to the next due to weather as well as the general state of the agricultural economy. Local, national and world supplies of commodities affect an individual producer's market. The impact of these variables may be localized or widespread. For example, deterioration in accounts receivable aging when compared to the prior year may indicate nothing more than the fact that farmers' planting season came earlier in the year due to more favorable weather conditions. Therefore, when developing expectations and evaluating the results of analytical procedures, the auditor needs to remain aware of both global and localized variables that impact the ratios and relationships being examined.

13.11 It is also important to understand the business practices of the audit client in comparison to other entities in similar lines of business. For example, different grain marketing cooperatives may follow differing practices for handling grain quality and moisture discounts, and may follow different practices for drying and blending grain. These practices will affect quantity shrinks and overruns as well as margins per unit. Changing government regulations may affect various practices as well, affecting environmental, labor, marketing, or other practices.

13.12 Unusual or unexpected relationships for agricultural cooperatives include the following:

- Inconsistent quantity shrinks or overruns in relation to industry peers, individual cooperative history, or blending/drying/operating practices
- Inconsistent unit margins in relation to industry peers, individual cooperative history, or blending/drying/operating practices
- Inconsistent unit sales in relation to general or local economic conditions or to local weather conditions
- Inconsistent reported profits in relation to economic and weather conditions
- Bad debt expense as a percent of sales more or less than industry peers or individual cooperative history
- Bad debt reserve as a percent of receivables more or less than industry peers or individual cooperative history
- Recorded receivables too high or too low in relation to sales
- Aging of receivables inconsistent with timing of peak season
- Total inventory out of line in relation to sales
- Inventory turnover, days sales in inventory, etc. inconsistent with peers, historic trends, or current economic conditions
- Operating expenses out of line in relation to gross income
- Payroll expenses per employee out of line with industry peers and historic trends

13.13 Agricultural producers may experience similar and other unusual or unexpected relationships, such as:

- Quality and net realizable value of the product harvested is unusual when compared to industry peers
- Debt ratios indicating tendency towards a more leveraged environment
- Inconsistent inventory levels relative to acreage harvested and collections prior to the end of the year
- "Repair" or "Supply" line items out of line with historical trends for the producer
- Repairs as a percentage of gross revenue increasing, possibly indicating financial pressures preventing upgrading of equipment
- Inventories of commodities relative to acreage planting indicating yields above the norm for the geographic area or crop
- Unexpected or unusually high "cullage" rates, compared to prior years or industry standards, may indicate the misappropriation of inventory
- Change in revenue per acre or revenue per unit harvested may be the result of poor marketing results or may indicate misappropriation
- Unusual results when compared to Farm Service Agency records of historical yields
- Deferred expenses for growing crops recorded at inappropriately high values per acre due to financial results pressures

13.14 The agricultural producer's mix of receivables, inventories and collections may vary drastically from year-to-year. Comparisons of beginning of the year receivables to receivables at the end of the year often are not meaningful. The same is true with inventories. However, the sum of receivables, inventories and post-harvest collections should bear similar relationships to total acreage harvested from year-to-year, taking into account weather and price variables. The auditor needs to be familiar with the weather patterns in the geographic area of the clients in order to properly evaluate the relationships in year-to-year comparisons. An understanding of the relationship of the local market price to national and world supply (how dependent the client's market is to national and world demand) is also necessary.

13.15 Auditors may also make inquiries of management to determine any unusual or unexpected relationships with customers, suppliers, board members, other members of management, and key employees.

Considering Fraud Risk Factors

13.16 As indicated in item 13.08c above, the auditor may identify events or conditions that indicate incentives/pressures to perpetrate fraud, opportunities to carry out the fraud, or attitudes/rationalizations to justify a fraudulent action. Such events or conditions are referred to as "fraud risk factors." Fraud risk factors do not necessarily indicate the existence of fraud; however, they often are present in circumstances where fraud exists.

13.17 SAS No. 99 provides fraud risk factor examples that have been written to apply to most enterprises. Paragraph 13.07 provides a list of fraud risk factors specific to the agricultural producers and cooperatives industry. Remember that fraud risk factors are only one of several sources of information an auditor considers when identifying and assessing risk of material misstatement due to fraud.

Identifying Risks That May Result in a Material Misstatement Due to Fraud

13.18 In identifying risks of material misstatement due to fraud, it is helpful for the auditor to consider the information that has been gathered in accordance with the requirements of paragraphs 19 through 34 of SAS No. 99. The auditor's identification of fraud risks may be influenced by characteristics such as the size, complexity, and ownership attributes of the entity. In addition, the auditor should evaluate whether identified risks of material misstatement due to fraud can be related to specific financial-statement account balances or classes of transactions and related assertions, or whether they relate more pervasively to the financial statements as a whole. Certain accounts, classes of transactions, and assertions that have high inherent risk because they involve a high degree of management judgment and subjectivity also may present risks of material misstatement due to fraud because they are susceptible to manipulation by management.

13.19 For example, in addition to their susceptibility to misappropriation, inventories of cooperatives and producers may be subject to fraudulent financial reporting involving the valuation and allocation assertion. Although the availability of reliable purchase or market prices may alleviate this concern, determination of net realizable value or lower-of-cost-or-market can be subjective and will often involve managerial estimates.

13.20 Equipment and other fixed assets are also vulnerable to misappropriation, but like inventory they can pose a risk of fraudulent financial reporting involving the valuation and allocation assertion. In particular, natural competitive pressures and changes in production technology make careful evaluation of possible impairment losses a critical management responsibility in the cooperative and producer environment. Given the broad range of factors that can influence this determination, estimation of any loss is likely to be highly subjective. The presentation and disclosure assertion may be relevant as well since impairment losses are reported in part according to management's plans for the underlying assets' use or disposition. For example, the producer may have a line of equipment unique to the harvesting of a particular crop. The market for the crop may have disappeared from the local area due to the closure of a processing plant. The producer will be sustaining the burden of switching to another crop, needing to acquire another line of equipment. The existing equipment may be idled, with no local or regional market for disposal of the equipment. The creditor's collateral may be impaired, even though the equipment is in good working condition. Apart from the possibility of such losses is the need to consider the impact of any asset retirement obligations that may exist with respect to property, plant, and equipment. Depending on the nature of the obligation, FASB Statement No. 143, *Accounting for Asset Retirement Obligations*, requires producers and cooperatives to estimate a fair value of the related liability for accrual and capitalization (and thus subsequent depreciation) purposes. Accordingly, rights and obligations becomes another assertion of possible audit concern in this area.

13.21 Valuation and allocation will again be an assertion of primary auditor interest in the area of cooperative investments, as will presentation and disclosure. Concern here is likely to center on carrying values and the effects of investee losses and unallocated equities. In this regard, management's interpretation and application of the relevant authoritative literature (e.g., APB Opinion No. 18) will require careful auditor consideration. The timing and recognition of patronage dividends may pose similar concerns. Furthermore, management's discretion in displaying patronage refunds suggests the need for auditor scrutiny since presentation choices (e.g., reductions of costs and expenses) made without adequate supporting disclosure may distort operating results.

13.22 The unique characteristics of cooperatives give rise to concern for the presentation and disclosure assertion in another financial statement area, specifically patrons' equities. In addition to determining that classifications are consistent with the underlying economic realities, the auditor should ascertain that allocated equities have been determined in accordance with the cooperative's bylaws and any statutory requirements. In this regard, the auditor should also consider the existence of due dates or interest obligations that would suggest the need to reclassify patronage allocations as debt, thus, causing both valuation and allocation and rights and obligations assertions to become of greater audit concern.[*]

13.23 In the case of agricultural producers, integrated livestock and row crop operations are particularly challenging to audit due to financial charac-

---

[*] In May 2003, the FASB issued FASB Statement of Financial Accounting Standards No. 150, *Accounting for Certain Financial Instruments With Characteristics of Both Liabilities and Equity*. This Statement establishes standards for how an issuer classifies and measures certain financial instruments with characteristics of both liabilities and equity. It requires that an issuer classify a financial instrument that is within its scope as a liability (or an asset in some circumstances). Many of those instruments were previously classified as equity.

This Standard may have a significant impact on financial statements of agricultural cooperatives. Retained allocated equities which are usually repaid to cooperative patrons over a specific number of years generally meet the definition of mandatorily redeemable financial instruments under FASB Statement No. 150 and as such may have to be reclassified as liabilities. As a result, some agricultural cooperatives may report significantly reduced equities and increased liabilities in their GAAP financial statements.

In November 2003, the FASB issued FASB Staff Position (FSP) FAS 150-3, which defers the effective date of the mandatorily redeemable provisions of FASB Statement No. 150 and all related FSPs for nonpublic entities as follows: (a) until fiscal periods beginning after December 15, 2004 for instruments that are mandatorily redeemable on fixed dates and (b) indefinitely, pending further FASB action, if the redemption date is not fixed or if the payout amount is variable and not based on an index. Readers should be alert to further developments.

teristics unique to the operations. Crops raised may be fed to the livestock, hiding crops diverted by employees. Thus, with respect to key assertions, the auditor will want to emphasize both the existence and completeness of these inventories, as well as their classification—presentation and disclosure assertion. Records of units harvested compared to livestock pounds sold may indicate feed conversion ratios out of line with industry standards. Each agricultural producer uses land for unique purposes depending upon crop rotation, geographic limitations, soil type, weather conditions, livestock integration, etc. It is this "uniqueness" that makes auditing agricultural producers particularly difficult. The auditor needs to use information gathered from sources other than internal records to determine which crops were raised on which ground, to determine expectations for quantities harvested. Comparisons with the producer's historical results may be the better indicator of current problems. "Common size" financial information (classification on a per acre or per unit harvested) may also disclose anomalies.

A Presumption That Improper Revenue Recognition Is a Fraud Risk

13.24 Material misstatements due to fraudulent financial reporting often result from an overstatement of revenues (for example, through premature revenue recognition or recording fictitious revenues) or an understatement of revenues (for example, through improperly shifting revenues to a later period). Therefore, the auditor should ordinarily presume that there is a risk of material misstatement due to fraud relating to revenue recognition (See paragraph 41 of SAS No. 99). Due to the nature of agriculture, improper revenue recognition is possible related to crop revenue.

13.25 Agricultural cooperatives and producers are increasingly using derivatives and other complex contracts for marketing agricultural commodities and for hedging associated risks. Some of these contracts include embedded derivatives or derivative-like features. In some cases, neither top management nor the accounting staff fully understand these contracts, related risks and the associated accounting ramifications. Improper accounting for such activities can easily result in income being moved between fiscal periods.

13.26 Significant year-end revenue accruals may be based on estimates and management judgments. Special audit attention should be given to the reasonableness of such revenue accruals. Quantity, quality and value of year-end commodity inventories, particularly those stored in bulk form, are subject to numerous estimates. The misstatement of inventory does not directly affect revenue, but it has a direct effect on cost of sales and periodic earnings. For example, the value of the inventory of livestock will depend upon the health of the animals, weight and estimated costs of disposal for animals of market size. The auditor needs to have the experience to evaluate the various factors that affect the value of inventory or consider using a specialist to evaluate the estimates provided by management (see SAS No. 73, *Using the Work of a Specialist*). Commodities in storage are also subject to manipulation by management. Merely computing the volume of grain in storage is not sufficient to establish the bona fides of the value. Grain placed at the top of the bin may be of high quality, hiding substandard grain subject to substantial dockage.

13.27 In addition to timing of revenue recognition, timing and consistency of expense recognition can be used to manipulate results of operations. For example, the decision to expense or capitalize certain expenditures can be made inconsistently from one year to the next for the purpose of smoothing net income. Expense accruals and allowances can likewise be used to manipulate net income.

A Consideration of the Risk of Management Override of Controls

13.28 Even if specific risks of material misstatement due to fraud are not identified by the auditor, there is a possibility that management override of controls could occur, and accordingly, the auditor should address that risk (see paragraph 57 of SAS No. 99) apart from any conclusions regarding the existence of more specifically identifiable risks. Specifically, the procedures described in paragraphs 58 through 67 of SAS No. 99 should be performed to further address the risk of management override of controls. These procedures include (1) examining journal entries and other adjustments for evidence of possible material misstatement due to fraud, (2) reviewing accounting estimates for biases that could result in material misstatement due to fraud, and (3) evaluating the business rationale for significant unusual transactions.

Key Estimates

13.29 The following significant estimates are common in agricultural cooperatives and producers:

- Allowances for uncollectible accounts
- Inventory valuation allowances for obsolescence
- Inventory valuation allowances for quality and foreign substances (e.g., weed seed)
- Valuation allowances for discounts in commodity inventories of substandard quality, resulting in reduced carrying values
- Receivables for rebates to be received in the future from suppliers based on past purchases of products such as herbicides and pesticides
- Environmental remediation liabilities
- Future settlements of customer complaints
- Volume discounts to be credited to customers in the future, based on past sales
- Potential impairments of long-lived assets, particularly plant and equipment
- Fair value of investments in non-publicly-traded entities such as other cooperatives, joint ventures, limited liability companies, etc.

Assessing the Identified Risks After Taking Into Account an Evaluation of the Entity's Programs and Controls That Address the Risks[*]

13.30 Auditors should comply with the requirements of paragraphs 43 through 45 of SAS No. 99 concerning an entity's programs and controls that

---

[*] In March 2004, the PCAOB issued Auditing Standard No. 2, *An Audit of Internal Control Over Financial Reporting Performed in Conjunction With an Audit of Financial Statements*. At the time of development of this edition of the Guide, this Standard was not approved by the SEC and was therefore not effective. If approved by the SEC, this Standard would apply to audits of issuers, as defined by the Sarbanes-Oxley Act, and other entities when prescribed by the rules of the SEC (collectively referred to as "issuers"). PCAOB Auditing Standard No. 2 establishes requirements that apply when an auditor is engaged to audit both an issuer's financial statements and management's assessment of the effectiveness of internal control over financial reporting. Auditing Standard No. 2 specifically addresses and emphasizes the importance of controls over possible fraud and requires the auditor to test controls specifically intended to prevent or detect fraud that is reasonably likely to result in material misstatement of the financial statements. See the Preface of this Guide for more detailed information. Registered public accounting firms must comply with the Standards of the PCAOB in connection with the preparation or issuance of any audit report on the financial statements of an issuer and in their auditing and related attestation practices. Registered public accounting firms auditing issuers should keep alert to final SEC approval of this PCAOB Standard.

address identified risks of material misstatement due to fraud. It is important for the auditor to remember that most agricultural producers and cooperatives are small and so generally lack many of the programs and controls that their larger corporate counterparts would be expected to have in place. In particular, they tend to exhibit the same vulnerabilities typical of small businesses, e.g., lack of segregation of duties and limited expertise in the key areas of finance, accounting, and internal auditing. Moreover, because their operations are usually directed by a single individual (i.e., a CEO or the general manager), they are often at greater risk of management override of whatever controls do exist.

13.31 Thus, the auditor should look for the following programs and controls but with an awareness that some of these features are likely to be found only within more sophisticated or control-conscious agricultural producers and cooperatives:

- An effective, functional board of directors has established and maintains a strong control environment by setting an appropriate "tone at the top."

- With respect to cooperative boards in particular, the directors demonstrate an understanding of the somewhat different challenges confronting the organization as compared to those in the investor-owned corporation. The cooperative exists to provide economic benefits to its members rather than to generate a return on the owners' investment. The absence of profit maximization as the primary charge to the governing board may alleviate some of the related pressure that often leads to fraud. Although the cooperative directors remain responsive to the desires of the member-users, they balance these concerns with the more important goal of maintaining high standards of ethical behavior, especially when those desires conflict.

- The board has developed a meaningful and carefully considered entity-wide code of conduct and has conveyed its philosophy and guidance to employees at all levels. Additionally, the board has emphasized the significance of this code through formal training and active enforcement.

- With respect to the cooperatives' codes, they describe appropriate policies covering all significant aspects of cooperative operations, especially those of particular relevance in this setting—conflicts of interests, external employee activities, and relationships with patrons and suppliers.

- The board has demonstrated its commitment to maintaining a strong control environment by taking an aggressive stance toward fraud prevention. Specifically, the board uses a proactive approach that includes identifying and eliminating (or at least reducing) opportunities for fraud throughout the organization.

- In cooperatives, this commitment is further evidenced by the board having hired management with the competence and expertise necessary to carry out its policies. These individuals share the board's concern for high ethical standards and they exhibit a zero-tolerance attitude toward fraud.

- Management in both agricultural producers and cooperatives implement and monitor control activities to address specific concerns, particularly controls (e.g., physical security) designed to deter and detect misappropriation of inventories and equipment. Within the cooperative setting, key controls include scrutiny of related party transactions given the ownership by and patronage with members that characterizes this environment.

- Consistent with the Committee of Sponsoring Organizations of the Treadway Commission's (COSO) internal control framework, producers and cooperatives emphasize the risk assessment and monitoring components with respect to those fraud-related vulnerabilities that are particularly acute in the agricultural industry. Specifically, directors and managers follow technological developments that could render inventories and equipment obsolete, study global or local economic trends that could threaten the viability of customers and members, and review operating results and key performance indicators that could reveal fraud (e.g., especially those pertaining to production and payroll).

- Agricultural entities with public ownership have formed audit committees that meet the requirements of the Sarbanes-Oxley Act of 2002, particularly with respect to composition and function. This latter dimension includes the creation of a system to gather and respond to fraud-related tips and complaints.

- Cooperatives maintain detailed records of varieties and tons delivered to the elevator, with detailed reconciliation to sales and other transfers out of the elevator. State commodity licensing agencies periodically audit the reports.

13.32 The auditor should consider whether such programs and controls mitigate the identified risks of material misstatement due to fraud or whether specific control deficiencies exacerbate the risks. After the auditor has evaluated whether the entity's programs and controls have been suitably designed and placed in operation, the auditor should assess these risks taking into account that evaluation. This assessment should be considered when developing the auditor's response to the identified risks of material misstatement due to fraud.

Responding to the Results of the Assessment

13.33 Paragraphs 46 through 67 of SAS No. 99 provide requirements and guidance about an auditor's response to the results of the assessment of the risks of material misstatement due to fraud. The auditor responds to risks of material misstatement due to fraud in the following three ways:

a.   A response that has an overall effect on how the audit is conducted—that is, a response involving more general considerations apart from the specific procedures otherwise planned (see paragraph 50 of SAS No. 99).

b.   A response to identified risks involving the nature, timing, and extent of the auditing procedures to be performed (see paragraphs 51 through 56 of SAS No. 99). Procedures that the auditor of an agricultural cooperative or producer should consider would include:
   - Review any reports filed with the Farm Services Agency regarding land under the control of the producer (owned or leased) for additional evidence of acreage in production and expected yield
   - Obtain data in the form of expected or historical results from the field personnel of chemical and fertilizer suppliers for comparison to recorded amounts
   - Devote special attention to cut-offs between fiscal periods
   - Use more substantive tests (e.g., inspection, confirmation, analysis and vouching of details) in lieu of analytical procedures
   - Perform substantive procedures at year-end rather than at an interim date

- Devote special attention to identifying and understanding various contracts used to market commodities and hedge related risks
- Confirm with external parties the existence and significant terms of derivatives and other complex contracts
- Identify significant balances based on estimates. Scrutinize carefully the underlying information and methods used by management in developing the estimates. Details may need to be confirmed with outside parties.

c.   A response involving the performance of certain procedures to further address the risk of material misstatement due to fraud involving management override of controls, given the unpredictable ways in which such override could occur (see paragraphs 57 through 67 of SAS No. 99 and paragraph 13.33*b* above).

Evaluating Audit Evidence

13.34   Paragraphs 68 through 78 of SAS No. 99 provide requirements and guidance for evaluating audit evidence. The auditor should evaluate whether analytical procedures that were performed as substantive tests or in the overall review stage of the audit indicate a previously unrecognized risk of material misstatement due to fraud. The auditor also should consider whether responses to inquiries throughout the audit about analytical relationships have been vague or implausible, or have produced evidence that is inconsistent with other evidential matter accumulated during the audit.

13.35   At or near the completion of fieldwork, the auditor should evaluate whether the accumulated results of auditing procedures and other observations affect the assessment of the risks of material misstatement due to fraud made earlier in the audit. As part of this evaluation, the auditor with final responsibility for the audit should ascertain that there has been appropriate communication with the other audit team members throughout the audit regarding information or conditions indicative of risks of material misstatement due to fraud.

Responding to Misstatements That May Be the Result of Fraud

13.36   When audit test results identify misstatements in the financial statements, the auditor should consider whether such misstatements may be indicative of fraud. See paragraphs 75 through 78 of SAS No. 99 for requirements and guidance about an auditor's response to misstatements that may be the result of fraud. If the auditor believes that misstatements are or may be the result of fraud, but the effect of the misstatements is not material to the financial statements, the auditor nevertheless should evaluate the implications, especially those dealing with the organizational position of the person(s) involved.

13.37   If the auditor believes that the misstatement is or may be the result of fraud, and either has determined that the effect could be material to the financial statements or has been unable to evaluate whether the effect is material, the auditor should:

    a.   Attempt to obtain additional evidential matter to determine whether material fraud has occurred or is likely to have occurred and, if so, its effect on the financial statements and the auditor's report thereon.[1]

    b.   Consider the implications for other aspects of the audit (see paragraph 76 of SAS No. 99).

    c.   Discuss the matter and the approach for further investigation with an appropriate level of management that is at least one level above those involved, and with senior management and the audit committee.[2]

    d.   If appropriate, suggest that the client consult with legal counsel.

13.38 The auditor's consideration of the risks of material misstatement and the results of audit tests may indicate such a significant risk of material misstatement due to fraud that the auditor should consider withdrawing from the engagement and communicating the reasons for withdrawal to the audit committee or others with equivalent authority and responsibility. The auditor may wish to consult with legal counsel when considering withdrawal from an engagement.

Communicating About Possible Fraud to Management, the Audit Committee, and Others

13.39 Whenever the auditor has determined that there is evidence that fraud may exist, that matter should be brought to the attention of an appropriate level of management. See paragraphs 79 through 82 of SAS No. 99 for further requirements and guidance about communications with management, the audit committee, and others.

Documenting the Auditor's Consideration of Fraud

13.40 Paragraph 83 of SAS No. 99 requires certain items and events to be documented by the auditor. Auditors should comply with those requirements.

Practical Guidance

13.41 The AICPA Practice Aid, *Fraud Detection in a GAAS Audit—SAS No. 99 Implementation Guide*, provides a wealth of information and help on complying with the provisions of SAS No. 99. Moreover, this Practice Aid provides an understanding of the differences between the requirements of SAS No. 99 and SAS No. 82, which was superseded by SAS No. 99. This Practice Aid is an Other Auditing Publication as defined in SAS No. 95, *Generally Accepted Auditing Standards* (AICPA, *Professional Standards*, vol. 1, AU sec. 150). Other Auditing Publications have no authoritative status; however, they may help the auditor understand and apply SASs.

---

[1] See SAS No. 58 for guidance on auditors' reports issued in connection with audits of financial statements.

[2] If the auditor believes senior management may be involved, discussion of the matter directly with the audit committee may be appropriate.

Appendix A

[*Reserved.*]

Appendix B

Illustrative Financial Statements

Illustrative Financial Statements of an Agricultural Producer[*]

The following financial statements illustrate one currently acceptable form of financial reporting for an agricultural producer accounting for inventories of growing crops, harvested crops, and cattle at the lower of cost or market. A separate statement of income, with supporting calculations, illustrates one method of reporting when inventories of harvested crops are carried at net realizable value. Other forms of financial statements are acceptable, and more or less information may be appropriate, depending on the circumstances. The amounts shown on the illustrative financial statements may not necessarily indicate customary relationships between accounts.

The notes to the illustrative financial statements are representative of the basic type of disclosure for an agricultural producer. Additional disclosures such as information concerning related-party transactions, subsequent events, pension plans, postretirement benefits other than pensions,[**],[***] postemployment

---

[*] These illustrative financial statements have not been updated to reflect the accounting and reporting requirements of FASB Statement No. 150, *Accounting for Certain Financial Instruments With Characteristics of Both Liabilities and Equity*. FASB Statement No. 150 affects the issuer's accounting for three types of freestanding financial instruments. One type is mandatorily redeemable shares, which the issuing company is obligated to buy back in exchange for cash or other assets. A second type, which includes put options and forward purchase contracts, involves instruments that do or may require the issuer to buy back some of its shares in exchange for cash or other assets. The third type of instruments that are liabilities under this Statement is obligations that can be settled with shares, the monetary value of which is fixed, tied solely or predominantly to a variable such as a market index, or varies inversely with the value of the issuers' shares. FASB Statement No. 150 does not apply to features embedded in a financial instrument that is not a derivative in its entirety. In addition to its requirements for the classification and measurement of financial instruments in its scope, FASB Statement No. 150 also requires disclosures about alternative ways of settling the instruments and the capital structure of entities, all of whose shares are mandatorily redeemable. Please refer to FASB Statement No. 150 and FASB Staff Position (FSP) FAS 150-3 for the effective date information.

[**] In December 2003, the FASB issued FASB Statement No. 132 (revised 2003), *Employers' Disclosures About Pensions and Other Postretirement Benefits*, that improves financial statement disclosures for defined benefit plans. This Statement revises employers' disclosures about pension plans and other postretirement benefit plans. It does not change the measurement or recognition of those plans required by FASB Statements No. 87, *Employers' Accounting for Pensions,* No. 88, *Employers' Accounting for Settlements and Curtailments of Defined Benefit Pension Plans and for Termination Benefits*, and No. 106, *Employers' Accounting for Postretirement Benefits Other Than Pensions*. This Statement retains the disclosure requirements contained in FASB Statement No. 132, *Employers' Disclosures About Pensions and Other Postretirement Benefits*, which it replaces. It requires additional disclosures to those in the original FASB Statement No. 132 about the assets, obligations, cash flows, and net periodic benefit cost of defined benefit pension plans and other defined benefit postretirement plans. The required information should be provided separately for pension plans and for other postretirement benefit plans.

The guidance is effective for fiscal years ending after December 15, 2003, and for quarters beginning after December 15, 2003.

[***] On December 8, 2003, the President signed the Medicare Prescription Drug, Improvement and Modernization Act of 2003 (the Act) into law. The Act introduces a prescription drug benefit under Medicare (Medicare Part D) as well as a federal subsidy to sponsors of retiree health care benefit plans that provide a benefit that is at least actuarially equivalent to Medicare Part D. Questions have arisen regarding whether an employer that provides postretirement prescription drug coverage (a plan) should recognize the effects of the Act on its accumulated postretirement benefit obligation (APBO) and net postretirement benefit costs and, if so, when and how to account for those effects.

(continued)

AAG-APC APP B

benefits, lease commitments, accounting changes, off-balance-sheet risks, concentrations of credit risk, and other matters that are not unique to agricultural producers may be required by generally accepted accounting principles.

These illustrative financial statements do not and are not intended to include items that should be accounted for under the requirements of FASB Statement No. 133, *Accounting for Derivative Instruments and Hedging Activities,* as amended by FASB Statements No. 137, *Accounting for Derivative Instruments and Hedging Activities—Deferral of the Effective Date,* No. 138, *Accounting for Certain Derivative Instruments and Certain Hedging Activities, an Amendment of FASB Statement No. 133,* and No. 149, *Amendment of Statement 133 on Derivative Instruments and Hedging Activities.* Practitioners should refer to FASB Statement No. 133 and related amendments for guidance on reporting derivative instruments and hedging activities.

(footnote continued)

In January 2004, the FASB issues FASB Staff Position (FSP) FAS 106-1, *Accounting and Disclosure Requirements Related to the Medicare Prescription Drug, Improvement and Modernization Act of 2003*, which permits a sponsor of a postretirement health care plan that provides a prescription drug benefit to make a one-time election to defer accounting for the effects of the Act. Regardless of whether a sponsor elects that deferral, the FSP requires certain disclosures pending further consideration of the underlying accounting issues.

In May 2004, the FASB issued FSP FAS 106-2, *Accounting and Disclosure Requirements Related to the Medicare Prescription Drug, Improvement and Modernization Act of 2003*, which provides guidance on the accounting for the effects of the Act for employers that sponsor postretirement health care plans that provide prescription drug benefits. This FSP also requires those employers to provide certain disclosures regarding the effect of the federal subsidy provided by the Act. When this FSP becomes effective, or upon earlier adoption if elected, it supersedes FSP FAS 106-1. Except for certain nonpublic entities, this FSP is effective for the first interim or annual period beginning after June 15, 2004. For a nonpublic entity, as defined in FASB Statement No. 87, *Employers' Accounting for Pensions,* that sponsors one or more defined benefit postretirement health care plans that provide prescription drug coverage but of which no plan has more than 100 participants, this FSP is effective for fiscal years beginning after December 15, 2004. Earlier application of this FSP is encouraged.

Independent Auditor's Report

The Stockholders and Board of Directors
Grain and Cattle Producer, Inc.

We have audited the accompanying balance sheets of Grain and Cattle Producer, Inc., as of August 31, 20X2 and 20X1, and the related statements of income and retained earnings and cash flows for the years then ended. These financial statements are the responsibility of the Company's management. Our responsibility is to express an opinion on these financial statements based on our audits.

We conducted our audits in accordance with auditing standards generally accepted in the United States of America.[*] Those standards require that we plan and perform the audit to obtain reasonable assurance about whether the financial statements are free of material misstatement. An audit includes examining, on a test basis, evidence supporting the amounts and disclosures in the financial statements. An audit also includes assessing the accounting principles used and significant estimates made by management, as well as evaluating the overall financial statement presentation. We believe that our audits provide a reasonable basis for our opinion.

In our opinion, the financial statements referred to above present fairly, in all material respects, the financial position of Grain and Cattle Producer, Inc., as of [at] August 31, 20X2 and 20X1, and the results of its operations and its cash flows for the years then ended in conformity with accounting principles generally accepted in the United States of America.

[Firm Signature]
Certified Public Accountants

City, State
October 18, 20X2

---

[*] For audits of issuers, as defined by the Sarbanes-Oxley Act, and other entities when prescribed by the rules of the Securities and Exchange Commission (collectively referred to as "issuers"), Public Company Accounting Oversight Board (PCAOB) Auditing Standard No. 1, *References in Auditors' Reports to the Standards of the Public Company Accounting Oversight Board*, proposes to replace this sentence with the following sentence: "We conducted our audits in accordance with the standards of the Public Company Accounting Oversight Board (United States)." On May 14, 2004, the SEC approved PCAOB Auditing Standard No. 1 and also issued an interpretive release to help with its implementation. The SEC's interpretive release is designed to assist the PCAOB, registrants, auditors and investors by, among other things, addressing certain transitional implementation issues and clarifying the impact of Auditing Standard No. 1 on existing references in the SEC rules and regulations to "generally accepted auditing standards." (See Release No. 33-8422 for more information.) The release specifies that effective May 24, 2004, references in SEC rules and staff guidance and in the federal securities laws to GAAS or to specific standards under GAAS, as they relate to issuers, should be understood to mean the standards of the PCAOB, plus any applicable rules of the SEC. Registered public accounting firms must comply with the Standards of the PCAOB in connection with the preparation or issuance of any audit report on the financial statements of an issuer and in their auditing and related attestation practices. See the Preface of this Guide for more information.

Exhibit B-1

Grain and Cattle Producer, Inc.

Balance Sheets

	August 31,	
	20X2	20X1
Assets		
Current assets		
Cash and cash equivalents	$ 112,000	$ 195,000
Receivables (Notes 1 and 2)	510,000	475,000
Inventories (Note 1)		
Feed and supplies	75,000	70,000
Grain	265,000	245,000
Cattle	410,000	445,000
Deposits and prepaid expenses	90,000	65,000
Total current assets	1,462,000	1,495,000
Investment (Note 1)	54,000	47,000
Property and equipment, net		
(Notes 1 and 3)	5,288,000	4,837,000
Total assets	$6,804,000	$6,379,000
Liabilities and Stockholders' Equity		
Current liabilities		
Notes payable (Note 4)	$ 200,000	$ 200,000
Accounts payable and accrued expenses	247,000	267,000
Deferred tax liability, net (Note 5)	17,722	13,514
Current maturities of long-term debt	250,000	200,000
Total current liabilities	714,722	680,514
Deferred tax liability, net (Note 5)	192,278	159,486
Long-term debt (Note 4)	3,020,000	2,925,000
Total liabilities	3,927,000	3,765,000
Stockholders' equity		
Common stock, $100 par, authorized and		
issued 5,000 shares	500,000	500,000
Retained earnings	2,377,000	2,114,000
	2,877,000	2,614,000
Total liabilities and stockholders' equity	$6,804,000	$6,379,000

The accompanying notes are an integral part of the financial statements.

Exhibit B-2

Grain and Cattle Producer, Inc.

Statements of Income[1] and Retained Earnings

	Years Ended August 31,	
	20X2	20X1
Revenue		
Grain	$2,365,000	$1,810,000
Cattle	1,110,000	1,378,000
Interest	15,000	17,000
Other	14,000	22,000
Total revenue	3,504,000	3,227,000
Costs and expenses		
Grain	1,395,000	1,090,000
Cattle	910,000	1,025,000
Interest expense	375,000	355,000
General and administrative expense	280,000	275,000
Total costs and expenses	2,960,000	2,745,000
Income before provision for taxes on income	544,000	482,000
Provision for taxes on income (Note 5)	251,000	227,000
Net income	293,000	255,000
Retained earnings, beginning of year	2,114,000	1,889,000
Dividends paid	(30,000)	(30,000)
Retained earnings, end of year	$2,377,000	$2,114,000
Basic earnings per share	$ 58.60	$ 51.00
Dividends per share	$ 6.00	$ 6.00

The accompanying notes are an integral part of the financial statements.

---

[1] FASB Statement No. 130, *Reporting Comprehensive Income*, establishes standards for the reporting and display of comprehensive income and its components. The Statement requires that all items that are required to be recognized under accounting standards as components of comprehensive income be reported in a financial statement that is displayed with the same prominence as other financial statements. The Statement does not require a specific format for that financial statement but requires that an enterprise display an amount representing total comprehensive income for the period in that financial statement. The Statement does not apply to an enterprise that has no items of other comprehensive income in any period presented.

Exhibit B-3

Grain and Cattle Producer, Inc.

Statements of Cash Flows

| | Years Ended August 31, | |
	20X2	20X1
Cash flows from operating activities:		
Net income	$ 293,000	$ 255,000
Adjustments to reconcile net income to net cash provided by operating activities:		
Depreciation	190,000	175,000
Deferred income tax	37,000	38,000
Gain on sale of property and equipment	(6,000)	(2,000)
Change in assets and liabilities:		
Decrease in receivables	55,000	(50,000)
Decrease (increase) in inventories	10,000	(70,000)
Increase in deposits and prepaid expenses	(25,000)	(15,000)
(Decrease)/Increase in accounts payable and accrued expenses	(20,000)	33,000
Net cash provided by operating activities	534,000	364,000
Cash flows from investing activities:		
Sale of property and equipment	90,000	72,000
Additions to property and equipment	(725,000)	(210,000)
Note receivable	(90,000)	—
Net cash used in investing activities	(725,000)	(138,000)
Cash flows from financing activities:		
Repayment of notes payable	—	(50,000)
Issuance of long-term debt	345,000	—
Repayment of long-term debt	(200,000)	(200,000)
Allocated retains—Central Supply Cooperative	(7,000)	(5,000)
Dividends	(30,000)	(30,000)
Net cash provided by (used in) financing activities	108,000	(285,000)
Net decrease in cash and cash equivalents	(83,000)	(59,000)
Cash and cash equivalents at beginning of year	195,000	254,000
Cash and cash equivalents at end of year	$ 112,000	$ 195,000
Supplemental disclosure of cash flow data:		
Cash paid during the years for:		
Interest (net of amounts capitalized)	$ 250,000	$ 225,000
Income taxes	$ 259,000	$ 220,000

The accompanying notes are an integral part of the financial statements.

Grain and Cattle Producer, Inc.
Notes to Financial Statements
Years Ended August 31, 20X2 and 20X1

1. Nature of Operations and Summary of Significant Accounting Policies

Nature of operations. The company is an agricultural producer principally involved in breeding cattle and growing wheat and corn. The company sells primarily to domestic wholesale and retail distributors.

Use of estimates. The preparation of financial statements in conformity with generally accepted accounting principles requires management to make estimates and assumptions that affect the reported amounts of assets and liabilities and disclosure of contingent assets and liabilities at the date of the financial statements and the reported amounts of revenues and expenses during the reporting period. Actual results could differ from those estimates.

Cash equivalents. The company considers all highly liquid investments with a maturity of three months or less when purchased to be cash equivalents.

Receivables. Receivables from cattle and grain sales are based on contracted prices. The company provides an allowance for doubtful accounts which is based upon a review of outstanding receivables, historical collection information, and existing economic conditions. Normal trade receivables are due 30 days after the date of sale. Trade receivables past due more than 120 days are considered delinquent. Delinquent receivables are written off based on individual credit evaluation and specific circumstances of the customer.

Inventories. Cattle inventories are stated at the lower of cost (first-in, first-out method) or market. Costs of raised cattle include proportionate costs of breeding, including depreciation of the breeding herd, plus the costs of maintenance through the balance sheet date. Purchased cattle are carried at purchase cost plus costs of maintenance through the balance sheet date.

Harvested grain inventories are stated at the lower of cost (first-in, first-out method) or market. Growing crops are valued at the lower of cost or estimated market.

Investment. The investment in Central Supply Cooperative (Central) represents equities allocated to Grain and Cattle Producer, Inc. (the Company), by Central as of Central's most recent fiscal year-end, plus an accrual at the Company's fiscal year-end for anticipated patronage allocations. The accrual is based on the expected percentage (1 percent in both 20X2 and 20X1) of Central's total patronage applied to Central's interim operating results. Patronage refunds are credited to operating expenses.

Property and equipment. Property and equipment are stated at cost. Breeding animals are carried at purchase costs or inventory transfer amounts equal to the lower of accumulated animal maintenance costs or market. Depreciation is provided over the estimated useful lives of the assets on a straight-line basis (see note 3). Renewals and betterments are charged to property accounts. Costs of maintenance and repairs that do not improve or extend asset lives are charged to expense.

Long-lived assets. Long-lived assets to be held and used are tested for recoverability whenever events or changes in circumstances indicate that the related carrying amount may not be recoverable. When required, impairment losses on assets to be held and used are recognized based on the fair value of the asset and long-lived assets to be disposed of by sale are reported at the lower of carrying amount or fair value less cost to sell.

Income taxes. Provisions for income taxes are based on taxes payable or refundable for the current year and deferred taxes on temporary differences between the amount of taxable income and pretax financial income and between the tax bases of assets and liabilities and their reported amounts in the financial statements. Deferred tax assets and liabilities are included in the financial statements at currently enacted income tax rates applicable to the period in which the deferred tax assets and liabilities are expected to be realized or settled as prescribed in FASB Statement No. 109, *Accounting for Income Taxes.* As changes in tax laws or rate are enacted, deferred tax assets and liabilities are adjusted through the provision for income taxes.

Basic earnings per share. Basic earnings per share of common stock were computed by dividing income available to common stockholders, by the weighted average number of common shares outstanding for the year. Diluted earnings per share are not presented because the Company has issued no dilutive potential common shares.

2. Receivables

Receivables are composed of the following:

	August 31,	
	20X2	20X1
Note secured, due January 20X3, interest at 12%	$ 90,000	
Grain receivables	100,000	$110,000
Livestock receivables	298,000	320,000
Price-later receivables	50,000	65,000
Other	10,000	15,000
Less: Allowance for doubtful accounts	(38,000)	(35,000)
	$510,000	$475,000

3. Property and Equipment

Property and equipment are stated at cost. A summary of the Company's facilities is shown below.

	August 31,		
	20X2	20X1	Useful Lives
Land	$3,678,000	$3,214,000	
Buildings and land improvements	840,000	800,000	5-40 years
Machinery and equipment	560,000	515,000	3-15 years
Feedlot facilities	285,000	270,000	10-25 years
Breeding herd	1,025,000	978,000	8 years
	6,388,000	5,777,000	
Less accumulated depreciation	1,100,000	940,000	
Property and equipment, net	$5,288,000	$4,837,000	

Depreciation charged against income for the years ended August 31, 20X2 and 20X1, amounted to $190,000 and $175,000, respectively.

Note: FASB Statement No. 144, *Accounting for the Impairment or Disposal of Long-Lived Assets*,[2] requires certain disclosures if an impairment loss is recognized for assets to be held and used. An example of such a disclosure is shown below:

> *Recently adopted environmental legislation has placed certain restrictions on the use of agricultural machinery and equipment owned and operated by the company. This circumstance has called into question the recoverability of the carrying amounts of these assets. As a result, pursuant to FASB Statement No. 144,* Accounting for the Impairment or Disposal of Long-Lived Assets, *an impairment loss of $X,XXX has been recognized for this equipment and included as a component of income before income taxes under the caption "General and Administrative expense." In calculating the impairment loss, fair value was determined by reviewing quoted market prices for current sales of similar equipment.*

4. Long-Term Debt and Short-Term Borrowings

Long-term debt. The long-term debt, which is collateralized by real estate, outstanding as of August 31, 20X2 and 20X1, is summarized below.

	August 31,	
	20X2	*20X1*
Payable in annual principal installments of $200,000 with final installment of $125,000 in 20Y6; interest at 11%	$2,925,000	$3,125,000
Payable in annual principal installments of $50,000 with final installment of $45,000 in 20X8; interest at 14.5%	345,000	
	3,270,000	3,125,000
Less amount due within one year	250,000	200,000
Balance, due after one year	$3,020,000	$2,925,000

Maturities of long-term debt for each of the five fiscal years subsequent to August 31, 20X2, are as follows.

20X3	$ 250,000
20X4	250,000
20X5	250,000
20X6	250,000
20X7	250,000
Total	$1,250,000

---

[2] A toolkit, *Auditing Fair Value Measurements and Disclosures: Allocations of the Purchase Price Under FASB Statement of Financial Accounting Standards No. 141,* Business Combinations, *and Tests of Impairment Under FASB Statements No. 142,* Goodwill and Other Intangible Assets, *and No. 144,* Accounting for the Impairment or Disposal of Long-Lived Assets, contains nonauthoritative guidance to help auditors understand and apply Statements on Auditing Standards when auditing fair value measurements and disclosures related to business combinations, goodwill and other intangible assets, and certain impairment situations. The guidance is illustrated in the context of a business combination since many of the key concepts and principles are revealed in this common business situation. However, the concepts and procedures described may also be useful when auditing goodwill and other intangible assets accounted for under FASB Statement No. 142 and when auditing impairment or disposal of assets accounted for under FASB Statement No. 144. Therefore, the illustrative audit program and illustrative disclosure checklist cover FASB Statements No. 142 and No. 144 in addition to FASB Statement No. 141. Additionally, the toolkit provides an overview of FASB Statements No. 142 and No. 144 and discusses certain auditing considerations. The toolkit is free and may be downloaded from www.aicpa.org/members/div/auditstd/fasb123002.asp.

The debt agreements contain a number of restrictive covenants on the payment of dividends including, among other things, a limit of 75 percent of the net earnings over $100,000 per year.

Short-term borrowings. The Company had a short-term line of credit with First National Bank of up to $300,000 in 20X2 and $250,000 in 20X1. The average interest rates were 17 percent and 18 percent for the years ended August 31, 20X2 and 20X1, respectively.

5. Income Taxes

The provision for income taxes consist of the following:

| | Years Ended August 31, | |
	20X2	20X1
Current		
Federal	$197,000	$175,000
State	17,000	14,000
Total current	214,000	189,000
Deferred		
Federal	28,000	30,000
State	9,000	8,000
Total deferred	37,000	38,000
Total	$251,000	$227,000

The net tax effects of temporary differences between the carrying amounts of assets and liabilities for financial reporting purposes and the amounts used for income tax purposes are reflected in deferred income taxes. Significant components of the company's deferred tax liabilities as of August 31, 20X2 and 20X1 are as follows:

| | Years Ended August 31, | |
	20X2	20X1
Current deferred tax assets/(liabilities)		
Inventory valuation methods	$ 5,523	$ 1,986
Capitalized costs	(23,245)	(15,500)
Total current deferred tax liability	$ (17,722)	$ (13,514)
Noncurrent deferred tax assets/(liabilities)		
Accelerated depreciation	(175,462)	(142,435)
Other, (net)	(16,816)	(17,051)
Total noncurrent deferred tax liability	$(192,278)	$(159,486)

A reconciliation of the income tax provision with amounts determined by applying the federal statutory rate to income before income taxes is as follows:

| | Years Ended August 31, | |
	20X2	20X1
Federal statutory income tax rate	34.0%	34.0%
State and local income tax	4.8	4.6
Nondeductible expenses	4.6	5.1
Other	2.7	3.4
Effective tax rate	46.1%	47.1%

6. Fair Value of Financial Instruments

The carrying amount of the company's current maturities of long-term debt approximate their fair value. The fair value of net long-term debt, which is based upon borrowing rates currently available to the company for debt issues with similar terms and maturities, is $2,895 (20X1, $2,640).[3, 4]

---

[3] FASB Statement No. 126, *Exemption From Certain Required Disclosures About Financial Instruments for Certain Nonpublic Entities, an Amendment of FASB Statement No. 107*, as amended by FASB Statements No. 133, *Accounting for Derivative Instruments and Hedging Activities*, and No. 149, *Amendment of Statement 133 on Derivative Instruments and Hedging Activities*, amends FASB Statement No. 107, *Disclosures About Fair Value of Financial Instruments*, to make the disclosures about fair value of financial instruments prescribed in FASB Statement No. 107 optional for entities that meet all of the following criteria:

    a. The entity is a nonpublic entity.

    b. The entity's total assets are less than $100 million on the date of the financial statements.

    c. The entity has no instrument that, in whole or in part, is accounted for as a derivative instrument under FASB Statement No. 133, other than commitments related to the origination of mortgage loans to be held for sale, during the reporting period.

[4] SAS No. 101, *Auditing Fair Value Measurements and Disclosures,* contains significantly expanded guidance on the audit procedures for fair value measurements and disclosures. Please refer to paragraphs 12.40–12.43 for a discussion of SAS No. 101.

Exhibit B-4

Grain and Cattle Producer, Inc.

Statements of Income

The presentation in exhibit B-5 illustrates the statements of income of Grain and Cattle Producer, Inc., with grain inventories valued at net realizable value.[5] The amounts included in the statement are based on the following cost and market amounts.

	20X2	20X1	20X0
Ending inventory at cost	$ 265,000	$ 245,000	$180,000
Ending inventory at net realizable value	$ 290,000	$ 263,000	$200,000
Cost of grain sold, with inventory stated at cost	$1,395,000	$1,090,000	
Adjusted for the change in the cost of inventories:			
for 20X2 ($265,000 less $245,000)	20,000	—	
for 20X1 ($245,000 less $180,000)	—	65,000	
Costs incurred for grain production	1,415,000	1,155,000	
Beginning inventory at net realizable value	263,000	200,000	
Ending inventory at net realizable value	(290,000)	(263,000)	
Cost of grain sold, with inventory stated at net realizable value	$1,388,000	$1,092,000	

---

[5] Paragraph 39 of SOP 85-3, *Accounting by Agricultural Producers and Agricultural Cooperatives* [Appendix C], provides the criteria necessary to value inventories of producers at sales price less estimated costs of disposal.

Exhibit B-5

Grain and Cattle Producer, Inc.
Alternative Statements of Income[6]

| | Years Ended August 31, | |
	20X2	20X1
Revenue		
Sales of grain	$2,365,000	$1,810,000
Sales of cattle	1,110,000	1,378,000
Interest	15,000	17,000
Other	14,000	22,000
Total revenue	3,504,000	3,227,000
Costs and expenses		
Grain	1,388,000	1,092,000
Cattle	910,000	1,025,000
Interest expense	375,000	355,000
General and administrative expense	280,000	275,000
Total costs and expenses	2,953,000	2,747,000
Income before income taxes	$ 551,000	$ 480,000

---

[6] This statement of income assumes grain inventories are accounted for at net realizable value.

Illustrative Financial Statements of Agricultural Cooperatives[7]

The following financial statements of cooperatives are included for illustrative purposes only and are not intended to establish reporting requirements. Furthermore, the dollar amounts shown are illustrative only and may not indicate any customary relationship among accounts. These financial statements do not include all the accounts and transactions that might be found in practice. The notes indicate the subject matter generally disclosed. In addition to the illustrative notes that are presented, some of which are peculiar to cooperatives, financial statements of cooperatives should include any other appropriate disclosures, such as information concerning related-party transactions, subsequent events, pension plans, postretirement benefits other than pensions,[*][**] postemployment benefits, lease commitments, accounting changes, off-balance-sheet risks, concentrations of credit risk, and other matters that are not unique to agricultural cooperatives. Certain disclosures included in the illustrative financial statements may not be required for nonpublic companies.

In the illustrative cooperative financial statements, it is assumed that the distribution of patronage proceeds or margins in cash and allocated equities is in accordance with appropriate action of the board of directors prior to the issuance of the financial statements. It is further assumed that amounts shown as allocated

---

[7] The staff of the SEC may require a different financial statement format in filings with the SEC depending on the particular circumstances.

[*] In December 2003, the FASB issued FASB Statement No. 132 (revised 2003), *Employers' Disclosures About Pensions and Other Postretirement Benefits*, that improves financial statement disclosures for defined benefit plans. This Statement revises employers' disclosures about pension plans and other postretirement benefit plans. It does not change the measurement or recognition of those plans required by FASB Statements No. 87, *Employers' Accounting for Pensions*, No. 88, *Employers' Accounting for Settlements and Curtailments of Defined Benefit Pension Plans and for Termination Benefits*, and No. 106, *Employers' Accounting for Postretirement Benefits Other Than Pensions*. This Statement retains the disclosure requirements contained in FASB Statement No. 132, *Employers' Disclosures About Pensions and Other Postretirement Benefits*, which it replaces. It requires additional disclosures to those in the original FASB Statement No. 132 about the assets, obligations, cash flows, and net periodic benefit cost of defined benefit pension plans and other defined benefit postretirement plans. The required information should be provided separately for pension plans and for other postretirement benefit plans.

The guidance is effective for fiscal years ending after December 15, 2003, and for quarters beginning after December 15, 2003.

[**] On December 8, 2003, the President signed the Medicare Prescription Drug, Improvement and Modernization Act of 2003 (the Act) into law. The Act introduces a prescription drug benefit under Medicare (Medicare Part D) as well as a federal subsidy to sponsors of retiree health care benefit plans that provide a benefit that is at least actuarially equivalent to Medicare Part D. Questions have arisen regarding whether an employer that provides postretirement prescription drug coverage (a plan) should recognize the effects of the Act on its accumulated postretirement benefit obligation (APBO) and net postretirement benefit costs and, if so, when and how to account for those effects.

In January 2004, the FASB issues FASB Staff Position (FSP) FAS 106-1, *Accounting and Disclosure Requirements Related to the Medicare Prescription Drug, Improvement and Modernization Act of 2003*, which permits a sponsor of a postretirement health care plan that provides a prescription drug benefit to make a one-time election to defer accounting for the effects of the Act. Regardless of whether a sponsor elects that deferral, the FSP requires certain disclosures pending further consideration of the underlying accounting issues.

In May 2004, the FASB issued FSP FAS 106-2, *Accounting and Disclosure Requirements Related to the Medicare Prescription Drug, Improvement and Modernization Act of 2003*, which provides guidance on the accounting for the effects of the Act for employers that sponsor postretirement health care plans that provide prescription drug benefits. This FSP also requires those employers to provide certain disclosures regarding the effect of the federal subsidy provided by the Act. When this FSP becomes effective, or upon earlier adoption if elected, it supersedes FSP FAS 106-1. Except for certain nonpublic entities, this FSP is effective for the first interim or annual period beginning after June 15, 2004. For a nonpublic entity, as defined in FASB Statement No. 87, *Employers' Accounting for Pensions,* that sponsors one or more defined benefit postretirement health care plans that provide prescription drug coverage but of which no plan has more than 100 participants, this FSP is effective for fiscal years beginning after December 15, 2004. Earlier application of this FSP is encouraged.

equities do not have attributes of debt, such as fixed due dates or interest bearing, that would suggest that those instruments be treated as liabilities.[†]

The financial statements for Midstate Marketing Cooperative (exhibits B-7 through B-11) have been prepared on the basis of charging cost of production for patrons' raw product deliveries, and valuing inventories of finished goods and goods in process at the lower of cost or market. However, for illustrative purposes certain statements for Midstate are presented (1) as if no value had been assigned to patrons' raw product deliveries and inventories of finished goods and goods in process had been valued at net realizable value (exhibits B-13 and B-14) and (2) as if cost of production had been charged for patrons' raw product deliveries and inventories of finished goods and goods in process had been valued at net realizable value (exhibit B-13). The above three methods are acceptable in accordance with paragraphs 83 through 85 of SOP 85-3.

In the accompanying illustrative statements of amounts due to patrons (exhibits B-9, B-14, and B-16) and the illustrative statements of net operations (exhibits B-8, B-13, and B-15), net proceeds are classified as to patronage and nonpatronage. For Midstate Marketing Cooperative (exhibit B-8) and Central Supply Cooperative (exhibit B-18), margins before income taxes are comparable with earnings of other corporate entities before income taxes.

Midstate Marketing Cooperative, as an agricultural marketing cooperative, differs from agricultural supply cooperatives and nonagricultural cooperatives because it receives agricultural products from its patrons, processes and markets those products, and returns to its patrons the patronage earnings in cash and allocated equities. Therefore an illustrative statement of amounts due to patrons is included showing an analysis of the distribution of the cooperative's patronage proceeds.

[†] In May 2003, the FASB issued FASB Statement of Financial Accounting Standards No. 150, *Accounting for Certain Financial Instruments With Characteristics of Both Liabilities and Equity*. This Statement establishes standards for how an issuer classifies and measures certain financial instruments with characteristics of both liabilities and equity. It requires that an issuer classify a financial instrument that is within its scope as a liability (or an asset in some circumstances). Many of those instruments were previously classified as equity.

This Standard may have a significant impact on the financial statements of agricultural cooperatives. Retained allocated equities which are usually repaid to cooperative patrons over a specific number of years generally meet the definition of mandatorily redeemable financial instruments under FASB Statement No. 150 and as such may have to be reclassified as liabilities. As a result, some agricultural cooperatives may report significantly reduced equities and increased liabilities in their GAAP financial statements. Cooperatives' balance sheets, statements of amounts due to patrons and statements of patrons' equities, as well as certain notes to financial statements, are likely to be affected.

In November 2003, the FASB issued FASB Staff Position (FSP) FAS 150-3, which defers the effective date of the mandatorily redeemable provisions of FASB Statement No. 150 and all related FSPs for nonpublic entities as follows: (a) until fiscal periods beginning after December 15, 2004 for instruments that are mandatorily redeemable on fixed dates and (b) indefinitely, pending further FASB action, if the redemption date is not fixed or if the payout amount is variable and not based on an index. Readers should be alert to further developments as cooperatives' financial statements may be significantly affected when the provisions of FASB Statement No. 150 for mandatorily redeemable financial instruments become effective.

Exhibit B-6

Midstate Marketing Cooperative
Balance Sheets[*]

| | April 30, | |
	20X2	20X1
Assets		
Current assets		
Cash and cash equivalents	$ 2,890,000	$ 6,360,000
Accounts receivable (Notes 1, 2, and 4)	13,120,000	9,600,000
Inventories (Notes 3 and 4)	35,050,000	30,980,000
Prepaid expenses and other current assets	1,170,000	1,370,000
Total current assets	52,230,000	48,310,000
Investment and other assets		
Investment in Bank for Cooperatives	6,200,000	5,340,000
Trademarks	1,600,000	2,000,000
Other assets	370,000	190,000
Total investments and other assets	8,170,000	7,530,000
Property, plant, and equipment (Note 4)		
Land	1,130,000	1,130,000
Buildings and improvements	10,970,000	10,860,000
Machines and equipment	25,280,000	19,760,000
Total property, plant, and equipment	37,380,000	31,750,000
Less accumulated depreciation	(13,670,000)	(12,170,000)
Net property, plant, and equipment	23,710,000	19,580,000
Total assets	$84,110,000	$75,420,000

(continued)

[*] See footnote † to the foreword to the Illustrative Financial Statements of Agricultural Cooperatives.

Exhibit B-6, continued

	April 30,	
	20X2	*20X1*
Liabilities and Patrons' Equities		
Current liabilities		
Notes payable to bank (Note 4)	$17,480,000	$16,950,000
Accounts payable and accrued expenses	8,100,000	7,480,000
Salaries, wages, and related payroll taxes	1,560,000	1,080,000
Due to patrons	10,260,000	8,910,000
Deferred tax liability, net (Note 5)	500,895	458,797
Current portion of long-term debt	2,890,000	2,890,000
Total current liabilities	40,790,895	37,768,797
Deferred tax liability, net (Note 5)	1,799,105	1,541,203
Long-term debt (Note 4)	13,210,000	16,100,000
Patrons' equities		
Allocated equities	26,360,000	19,710,000
Unallocated equities	1,950,000	300,000
	28,310,000	20,010,000
Total liabilities and patrons' equities	$84,110,000	$75,420,000

The accompanying notes are an integral part of the financial statements.

Exhibit B-7

Midstate Marketing Cooperative
Statements of Operations[8]

| | Years Ended April 30, | |
	20X2	20X1
Net sales	$129,630,000	$110,110,000
Expenses		
Cost of sales (including proportionate share of assigned value of patrons' raw products received)	84,630,000	70,200,000
Selling, general, and administrative expense	19,380,000	18,900,000
Interest expense	5,090,000	4,750,000
Total expenses	109,100,000	93,850,000
Proceeds before provision for taxes on income	20,530,000	16,260,000
Provision for taxes on income (Note 5)	1,250,000	900,000
Net proceeds	$ 19,280,000	$ 15,360,000
Patronage	17,630,000	14,100,000
Nonpatronage	1,650,000	1,260,000
	$ 19,280,000	$ 15,360,000

The accompanying notes are an integral part of the financial statements.

---

[8] FASB Statement No. 130, *Reporting Comprehensive Income*, establishes standards for the reporting and display of comprehensive income and its components. The Statement requires that all items that are required to be recognized under accounting standards as components of comprehensive income be reported in a financial statement that is displayed with the same prominence as other financial statements. The Statement does not require a specific format for that financial statement but requires that an enterprise display an amount representing total comprehensive income for the period in that financial statement. The Statement does not apply to an enterprise that has no items of other comprehensive income in any period presented.

Exhibit B-8

Midstate Marketing Cooperative
Statements of Amounts Due to Patrons*

	April 30,	
	20X2	*20X1*
Amounts due to patrons at beginning of year	$ 8,910,000	$ 9,070,000
Assigned value of patrons' raw products (approximates market at date of receipt)	56,500,000	51,500,000
Net patronage proceeds	17,630,000	14,100,000
Total	83,040,000	74,670,000
Less:		
Amounts paid to patrons in cash	58,830,000	53,240,000
Amounts retained as:		
Per-unit retains	5,650,000	5,250,000
Equity credits	8,300,000	7,270,000
Total	72,780,000	65,760,000
Amounts due to patrons at end of year	$10,260,000	$ 8,910,000

The accompanying notes are an integral part of the financial statements.

---

* See footnote † to the foreword to the Illustrative Financial Statements of Agricultural Cooperatives.

Exhibit B-9

Midstate Marketing Cooperative

Statements of Patrons' Equities[*]

| | Allocated | | | Unallocated |
	Equity Credits	Per-Unit Retains	Total	Equities (Deficit)
Balance, April 30, 20X0	$ 8,730,000	$ 5,210,000	$13,940,000	$ (960,000)[9]
Patronage proceeds	7,270,000	—	7,270,000	—
Refund of prior years' allocated equities	(6,750,000)	—	(6,750,000)	—
Per-unit retains	—	5,250,000	5,250,000	—
Nonpatronage proceeds	—	—	—	1,260,000
Balance, April 30, 20X1	9,250,000	10,460,000	19,710,000	300,000
Patronage proceeds	8,300,000	—	8,300,000	—
Refund of prior years' allocated equities	(7,300,000)	—	(7,300,000)	—
Per-unit retains	—	5,650,000	5,650,000	—
Nonpatronage proceeds	—	—	—	1,650,000
Balance, April 30, 20X2	$10,250,000	$16,110,000	$26,360,000	$ 1,950,000

The accompanying notes are an integral part of the financial statements.

---

[*] See footnote † to the foreword to the Illustrative Financial Statements of Agricultural Cooperatives.

[9] Central Supply Cooperative, a patron of Midstate Marketing Cooperative, did not record its proportionate share of its investee's unallocated loss because of the assumption that the interim financial statements and projections reflected nonpatronage proceeds sufficient to offset the loss.

Exhibit B-10

Midstate Marketing Cooperative

Statements of Cash Flows

| | Years Ended April 30, | |
	20X2	20X1
Cash flows from operating activities:		
Net proceeds	$19,280,000	$15,360,000
Adjustments to reconcile net proceeds to net cash provided by operating activities:		
Depreciation and amortization	3,500,000	3,200,000
Provisions for losses on accounts receivable	50,000	(10,000)
Deferred income taxes	300,000	160,000
Change in noncash current assets and liabilities:		
Accounts receivable	(3,570,000)	660,000
Inventories	(4,070,000)	(1,100,000)
Prepaid expenses and other current assets	200,000	(250,000)
Accounts payable and accrued expenses	620,000	580,000
Salaries, wages, and related payroll taxes	480,000	(220,000)
Amounts due to patrons	1,350,000	400,000
Net cash provided by operating activities	18,140,000	18,780,000
Cash flows from investing activities:		
Property, plant, and equipment additions	(7,230,000)	(5,440,000)
Investments and other assets	(1,040,000)	(520,000)
Net cash used in investing activities	(8,270,000)	(5,960,000)
Cash flows from financing activities:		
Repayment of long-term debt	(2,890,000)	(2,890,000)
Increase in notes payable to bank	530,000	1,000,000
Per-unit retains	5,650,000	5,250,000
Patronage distributions	(9,330,000)	(6,830,000)
Payment of prior years' retains	(7,300,000)	(6,750,000)
Net cash used in financing activities	(13,340,000)	(10,220,000)
Net Change in cash and cash equivalents	(3,470,000)	2,600,000
Cash and cash equivalents at beginning of year	6,360,000	3,760,000
Cash and cash equivalents at end of year	$ 2,890,000	$ 6,360,000
Supplemental disclosure of cash flow data:		
Cash paid during the years for:		
Interest (net of amounts capitalized)	$ 5,500,000	$ 5,250,000
Income taxes	$ 1,300,000	$ 800,000

The accompanying notes are an integral part of the financial statements.

Midstate Marketing Cooperative

Notes to Financial Statements

Years Ended April 30, 20X2 and 20X1

1. Nature of Operations and Summary of Significant Accounting Policies

Nature of operations. Midstate Marketing Cooperative is an agricultural cooperative association operating on a pool basis, and it is organized for the purpose of processing and marketing fruits and vegetables delivered by its patrons who are principally agricultural producers located in the Midwestern region of the United States. Deliveries from nonmember growers may also be accepted on a patronage or nonpatronage basis. Patrons are credited for the assigned amounts (as determined by the board of directors) of raw products delivered. Net proceeds or losses from patronage business are allocated to patrons on the basis of their participation in the total established value of the related pool.

Use of estimates. The preparation of financial statements in conformity with generally accepted accounting principles requires management to make estimates and assumptions that affect the reported amounts of assets and liabilities and disclosure of contingent assets and liabilities at the date of the financial statements and the reported amounts of revenues and expenses during the reporting period. Actual results could differ from those estimates.

Equity requirements, as determined by the board of directors, are retained from amounts due to patrons and credited to patrons' equity.

Unallocated equities arising from nonpatronage business and certain nonrecurring revenues and expenses, less income taxes, are not allocated to patrons.

Cash equivalents. The cooperative considers all highly liquid investments with a maturity of three months or less when purchased to be cash equivalents.

Accounts receivable. Receivables from fruits and vegetables sales are based on contracted prices. The company provides an allowance for doubtful accounts which is based upon a review of outstanding receivables, historical collection information, and existing economic conditions. Normal trade receivables are due 30 days after the date of sale. Trade receivables past due more than 120 days are considered delinquent. Delinquent receivables are written off based on individual credit evaluation and specific circumstances of the customer.

Inventories. The cooperative's inventories are stated at the lower of cost or market using the first-in, first-out method (FIFO). Raw products received from members are included as an element of cost at their assigned amounts.

Investments. The investment in the Bank for Cooperatives consists of class C stock at cost and the cooperative's share of the bank's allocated surplus. Patronage refunds are credited to interest expense.

Trademarks. Purchase costs of trademarks are capitalized and amortized over ten years.

Property, plant, and equipment. Property, plant, and equipment are stated at cost. Depreciation is computed principally by using the straight-line method over the estimated useful lives of the related depreciable assets. Expenditures for betterments and renewals that extend useful lives are capitalized. Gains and losses on retirements and disposals are included in net proceeds.

Long-lived assets. Long-lived assets to be held and used are tested for recoverability whenever events or changes in circumstances indicate that the related carrying amount may not be recoverable. When required, impairment losses on assets to be held and used are recognized based on the fair value of the asset and long-lived assets to be disposed of by sale are reported at the lower of carrying amount or fair value less cost to sell.

*Patrons' equities.** In accordance with its bylaws, the cooperative allocates patronage proceeds to patrons, as determined for income tax purposes, in cash and equity certificates in proportions determined by its board of directors.

Income taxes. The cooperative, as a nonexempt cooperative, is taxed on nonpatronage proceeds and any patronage proceeds not paid or allocated to patrons. Provisions for income taxes are based on taxes payable or refundable for the current year and deferred taxes on temporary differences between the amount of taxable income and pretax financial income and between the tax bases of assets and liabilities and their reported amounts in the financial statements. Deferred tax assets and liabilities are included in the financial statements at currently enacted income tax rates applicable to the period in which the deferred tax assets and liabilities are expected to be realized or settled as prescribed in FASB Statement No. 109, *Accounting for Income Taxes.* As changes in tax laws or rate are enacted, deferred tax assets and liabilities are adjusted through the provision for income taxes.

2. Accounts Receivable

Receivables are composed of the following:

	April 30,	
	20X2	*20X1*
Fruit receivables	$7,485,000	$5,530,000
Vegetable receivables	6,110,000	4,500,000
Other	25,000	20,000
Less: Allowance for doubtful accounts	(500,000)	(450,000)
	$13,120,000	$ 9,600,000

3. Inventories

A summary of inventories follows.

	April 30,	
	20X2	*20X1*
Finished goods	$28,040,000	$22,820,000
Goods in process	4,320,000	5,560,000
Materials and supplies	2,690,000	2,600,000
Total	$35,050,000	$30,980,000

---

* See footnote † to the foreword to the Illustrative Financial Statements of Agricultural Cooperatives.

4. Notes Payable to Bank and Long-Term Debt

Notes payable to bank consist of short-term loans from the Bank for Cooperatives. Following is a summary of such borrowings during the years ended April 30, 20X2 and 20X1.

	April 30,	
	20X2	20X1
Borrowings as of April 30	$17,480,000	$16,950,000
Average interest rate on year-end borrowings	17.5%	13%
Average borrowings during the year	$19,500,000	$16,500,000
Average interest rate on borrowings during the year	15.75%	14.5%
Maximum borrowings during the year	$20,060,000	$25,000,000

Long-term debt consists of notes payable to the Bank for Cooperatives, which bear interest at 12.5 percent. Payments are due in varying installments through 20X8. Aggregate annual principal payments applicable to long-term debt for years subsequent to April 30, 20X2 are as follows.

Year Ending April 30,	
20X3	$ 2,890,000
20X4	2,890,000
20X5	2,890,000
20X6	2,890,000
20X7	2,270,000
Thereafter	2,270,000
Total	$16,100,000

Essentially, all accounts receivable and inventories are pledged as collateral under the short-term agreement.

The long-term notes are secured by property, plant, and equipment with a net book value of $18 million and by the investment in the Bank for Cooperatives.

The debt agreements with the Bank contain a number of restrictive covenants, including limitations on equipment purchases and prior approval of the Bank on revolvement of retained equities.[*]

---

[*] FASB Statement No. 150, *Accounting for Certain Financial Instruments With Characteristics of Both Liabilities and Equity*, may have a significant impact on debt covenants by reducing the cooperative's reported capital. See footnote † to the foreword to the Illustrative Financial Statements of Agricultural Cooperatives for the discussion of FASB Statement No. 150.

5. Income Taxes

The provision for income taxes consists of the following:

| | Years Ended April 30, | |
	20X2	20X1
Current		
Federal	$ 790,000	$470,000
State	160,000	100,000
Total current	950,000	570,000
Deferred		
Federal	250,000	270,000
State	50,000	60,000
	300,000	330,000
Total deferred	$1,250,000	$900,000

The net tax effects of temporary differences between the carrying amounts of assets and liabilities for financial reporting purposes and the amounts used for income tax purposes are reflected in deferred income taxes. Significant components of the cooperative's deferred tax liabilities as of April 30, 20X2 and 20X1 are as follows:

| | Years Ended April 30, | |
	20X2	20X1
Current deferred tax assets/(liabilities)		
Inventory valuation methods	$ 22,105	$ 28,203
Capitalized costs	(523,000)	(487,000)
Total current deferred tax liability	$ (500,895)	$ (458,797)
Noncurrent deferred tax assets/(liabilities)		
Accelerated depreciation	(1,762,289)	(1,523,152)
Other, (net)	(36,816)	(18,051)
Total noncurrent deferred tax liability	$(1,799,105)	$(1,541,203)

A reconciliation of the income tax provision with amounts determined by applying the federal statutory rate to income before income taxes is as follows:

| | Years Ended August 31, | |
	20X2	20X1
Federal statutory income tax rate	35.0%	35.0%
Qualified patronage distributions	(34.3)	(31.7)
State and local income tax	10.0	9.8
Other (net)	(4.6)	(7.6)
Effective tax rate	6.1%	5.5%

6. Fair Value of Financial Instruments

The carrying amount of the cooperative's current portion of long-term debt, approximates its fair value. The fair value of net long-term debt, which is based upon borrowing rates currently available to the Company for debt issues with similar terms and maturities, is $13,125 (20X1, $15,843).[10, 11]

---

[10] FASB Statement No. 126, *Exemption From Certain Required Disclosures About Financial Instruments for Certain Nonpublic Entities, an Amendment of FASB Statement No. 107,* as amended by FASB Statements No. 133, *Accounting for Derivative Instruments and Hedging Activities,* and No. 149, *Amendment of Statement 133 on Derivative Instruments and Hedging Activities,* amends FASB Statement No. 107, *Disclosures About Fair Value of Financial Instruments,* to make the disclosures about fair value of financial instruments prescribed in FASB Statement No. 107 optional for entities that meet all of the following criteria:

    a. The entity is a nonpublic entity.

    b. The entity's total assets are less than $100 million on the date of the financial statements.

    c. The entity has no instrument that, in whole or in part, is accounted for as a derivative instrument under FASB Statement No. 133, other than commitments related to the origination of mortgage loans to be held for sale, during the reporting period.

[11] SAS No. 101, *Auditing Fair Value Measurements and Disclosures,* contains significantly expanded guidance on the audit procedures for fair value measurements and disclosures. Please refer to paragraphs 12.40–12.43 for a discussion of SAS No. 101.

Exhibit B-11

Midstate Marketing Cooperative
Statements of Operations[12]

	Years Ended April 30,	
	20X2	20X1
Net sales	$129,630,000	$110,110,000
Product inventory, ending	35,596,000	31,218,000
Product inventory, beginning	(31,218,000)	(24,200,000)
Gross proceeds	134,008,000	117,128,000
Cost and expenses		
Processing and packing	32,110,000	25,080,000
Selling, general, and administrative expenses	19,380,000	18,900,000
Interest expense	5,090,000	4,750,000
	56,580,000	48,730,000
Proceeds before income taxes	77,428,000	68,398,000
Income taxes (Note 5)	1,250,000	900,000
Net proceeds	$ 76,178,000	$ 67,498,000
Patronage	$ 74,528,000	$ 66,238,000
Nonpatronage	1,650,000	1,260,000
	$ 76,178,000	$ 67,498,000

---

[12] In this example, no charge to cost of production has been made for patrons' raw product deliveries, and inventories of finished goods and goods in process have been valued at net realizable value.

Midstate Marketing Cooperative
Statements of Amounts Due to Patrons[*],[13]

	Years Ended April 30,	
	20X2	20X1
Amounts due to patrons at beginning of year	$11,748,000	$11,270,000
Net patronage proceeds	74,528,000	66,238,000
	86,276,000	77,508,000
Less:		
Amounts paid to patrons in cash	58,830,000	53,240,000
Amounts retained as:		
Per-unit retains	5,650,000	5,250,000
Equity credits	8,300,000	7,270,000
	72,780,000	65,760,000
Amounts due to patrons at end of year	$13,496,000	$11,748,000

---

[*] See footnote † to the foreword to the Illustrative Financial Statements of Agricultural Cooperatives.

[13] The amounts due to patrons at the end of the year are the same as shown in the financial statements in which cost of production has been charged for patrons' raw product deliveries and inventories of finished goods and goods in process have been valued at the lower of cost or market, except for the difference in valuing those inventories at the end of the year. The amounts due patrons are reconciled as follows:

Amounts due to patrons, with inventories valued at the lower of cost or market	$ 10,260,000	$ 8,910,000
Add adjustments of inventories to net realizable value	3,236,000	2,838,000
Amounts due patrons, with inventories valued at net realizable value	$ 13,496,000	$ 11,748,000

Inventories. Product inventories are stated at estimated net realizable values, determined by reducing sales value for completion, direct distribution, and selling costs. Supply inventories are stated at the lower cost or market using the first-in, first-out method (FIFO). Inventories consist of the following:

	April 30,	
	20X2	20X1
Finished goods	$30,844,000	$25,102,000
Goods in process	4,752,000	6,116,000
Materials and supplies	2,690,000	2,600,000
Total	$38,286,000	$33,818,000

Exhibit B-13

Midstate Marketing Cooperative
Statements of Operations[14]

	Years Ended April 30,	
	20X2	*20X1*
Net sales	$129,630,000	$110,110,000
Expenses		
Costs of sales (including proportionate share of assigned value of patrons' raw products received)	84,232,000	69,562,000
Selling, general, and administrative expense	19,380,000	18,900,000
Interest expense	5,090,000	4,750,000
Total expenses	108,702,000	93,212,000
Proceeds before income taxes	20,928,000	16,898,000
Provision for taxes on income (Note 5)	1,250,000	900,000
Net proceeds	$ 19,678,000	$ 15,998,000
Patronage	$ 18,028,000	$ 14,738,000
Nonpatronage	1,650,000	1,260,000
	$ 19,678,000	$ 15,998,000

---

[14] In determining net proceeds in this example, charges to cost of production, in the amounts of $56,500,000 and $51,500,000 for 20X2 and 20X1, respectively, have been made for patrons' raw product deliveries, with corresponding credits to amounts due to patrons. Inventories have been valued at net realizable value.

Exhibit B-14

Midstate Marketing Cooperative
Statements of Amounts Due to Patrons[*], [15]

	April 30,	
	20X2	20X1
Amounts due to patrons at beginning of year	$11,748,000	$11,270,000
Net patronage proceeds	18,028,000	14,738,000
Assigned value of patrons' raw product	56,500,000	51,500,000
Total	86,276,000	77,508,000
Less:		
Amounts paid to patrons in cash	58,830,000	53,240,000
Amounts retained as:		
Per-unit retains	5,650,000	5,250,000
Equity credits	8,300,000	7,270,000
	72,780,000	65,760,000
Amounts due to patrons at end of year	$13,496,000	$11,748,000

---

[*] See footnote † to the foreword to the Illustrative Financial Statements of Agricultural Cooperatives.

[15] The amounts due to patrons at the end of the year are the same as shown in the financial statements in which cost of production has been charged for patrons' raw product deliveries, and inventories of finished goods and goods in process have been valued at the lower of cost or market, except for the difference in valuing those inventories at the end of the year. Further, the amounts due members at the end of the year are the same as shown in the example in which cost of production has not been charged for cost of production and inventories of finished goods and goods in process have been valued at net realizable value.

The amounts due patrons under the two methods of inventory valuation are reconciled as follows:

	April 30,	
	20X2	20X1
Amounts due to patrons, with inventories valued at the lower of cost or market	$ 10,260,000	$ 8,910,000
Add adjustment of inventories to net realizable value	3,236,000	2,838,000
Amounts due patrons, with inventories valued at net realizable value	$ 13,496,000	$ 11,748,000

Inventories. Product inventories are stated at estimated net realizable values, determined by reducing sales value for completion, direct distribution, and selling costs. Supply inventories are stated at the lower cost or market using the first-in, first-out method (FIFO).

Inventories consist of the following:

	April 30,	
	20X2	20X1
Finished goods	$ 30,844,000	$ 25,102,000
Goods in process	4,752,000	6,116,000
Materials and supplies	2,690,000	2,600,000
Total	$ 38,286,000	$ 33,818,000

Exhibit B-15

Central Supply Cooperative
Balance Sheets[*]

	May 31,	
	20X2	*20X1*
Assets		
Current assets		
Cash and cash equivalents	$2,650,000	$2,819,000
Accounts receivable (Notes 1, 2, and 4)	6,573,000	6,298,000
Inventories (Notes 3 and 4)	15,520,000	14,686,000
Advances on grain purchases and margin deposits	1,240,000	1,610,000
Prepaid expenses and other current assets	1,195,000	1,306,000
Total current assets	27,178,000	26,719,000
Investments and other assets		
Investment in Midstate Marketing Cooperative	1,357,000	1,020,000
Investment in Bank for Cooperatives	1,274,000	1,160,000
Investment in Farm Fertilizers, Inc.	980,000	908,000
Other assets	126,000	192,000
	3,737,000	3,280,000
Property, plant, and equipment (Note 4)		
Land and land improvements	1,248,000	1,736,000
Buildings and improvements	10,753,000	9,726,000
Machinery and equipment	20,154,000	17,622,000
Automobiles and trucks	1,197,000	1,173,000
	33,352,000	30,257,000
Less accumulated depreciation	(10,165,000)	(8,247,000)
Net property, plant, and equipment	23,187,000	22,010,000
Total assets	$54,102,000	$52,009,000

(continued)

[*] See footnote † to the foreword to the Illustrative Financial Statements of Agricultural Cooperatives.

Exhibit B-15, continued

	May 31,	
	20X2	20X1
Liabilities and Patrons' Equities		
Current liabilities		
Notes payable to bank (Note 4)	$ 7,084,000	$ 6,473,000
Accounts payable and accrued expenses	10,994,000	11,045,000
Salaries, wages, and related payroll taxes	2,230,000	1,985,000
Patronage refunds payable	874,000	619,000
Deferred tax liability, net (Note 5)	126,200	177,500
Current portion of long-term debt	560,000	1,230,000
Total current liabilities	21,868,200	21,529,500
Deferred tax liability, net (Note 5)	1,400,800	1,176,500
Long-term debt (Note 4)	8,978,000	10,208,000
Commitments and contingencies (Note 6)		
Patrons' equities		
Preferred stock, 6% noncumulative, $100 par value: Authorized, 100,000 shares		
Issued and outstanding, 54,840 and 37,380 shares	5,484,000	3,738,000
Common stock, voting, $100 par value: Authorized, 25,000 shares		
Issued and outstanding, 5,070 and 5,020 shares	507,000	502,000
Allocated equities	13,650,000	13,632,000
Unallocated equities	2,214,000	1,223,000
Total patrons' equities	21,855,000	19,095,000
Total liabilities and patrons' equities	$54,102,000	$52,009,000

The accompanying notes are an integral part of the financial statements.

Exhibit B-16

Central Supply Cooperative
Statements of Operations

| | Years Ended May 31, | |
	20X2	20X1
Revenues		
Farm supply sales	$ 71,681,000	$ 67,391,000
Farm marketing sales	37,939,000	32,963,000
Other	1,055,000	978,000
	110,675,000	101,332,000
Costs and expenses		
Costs of raw materials, operations, and distribution	98,509,000	91,589,000
General and administrative expense	3,149,000	2,913,000
Interest expense	2,785,000	2,610,000
	104,443,000	97,112,000
Margins before provision for taxes on income	6,232,000	4,220,000
Provision for taxes on income (Note 6)	650,000	545,000
Net margins	$ 5,582,000	$ 3,675,000
Net patronage margins to be distributed as follows:		
Cash	$ 874,000	$ 619,000
Preferred stock	1,746,000	1,238,000
Allocated equities	1,747,000	1,238,000
	4,367,000	3,095,000
Nonpatronage margins to unallocated equities	1,215,000	580,000
	$ 5,582,000	$ 3,675,000

The accompanying notes are an integral part of the financial statements.

Exhibit B-17

Central Supply Cooperative
Statements of Patrons' Equities[*]

	Preferred Stock	Allocated Common Stock	Allocated Equities	Unallocated Margins
Balance, May 31, 20X0	$2,500,000	$500,000	$15,268,000	$ 793,000
Patronage margins	1,238,000		1,238,000	
Refund of prior years' allocated equities			(2,874,000)	
Net nonpatronage margins				580,000
Preferred stock dividends				(150,000)
New memberships, net		2,000		
Balance, May 31, 20X1	3,738,000	502,000	13,632,000	1,223,000
Patronage margins	1,746,000		1,747,000	
Refund of prior years' allocated equities			(1,729,000)	
Nonpatronage margins				1,215,000
Preferred stock dividends				(224,000)
New memberships, net		5,000		
Balance, May 31, 20X2	$5,484,000	$507,000	$13,650,000	$2,214,000

The accompanying notes are an integral part of the financial statements.

[*] See footnote † to the foreword to the Illustrative Financial Statements of Agricultural Cooperatives.

Exhibit B-18

Central Supply Cooperative
Statements of Cash Flows

	Years Ended May 31,	
	20X2	*20X1*
Cash flows from operating activities:		
Net margins	$ 5,582,000	$ 3,675,000
Noncash items included in net margins:		
Depreciation and amortization	2,937,000	2,537,000
Provisions for losses on accounts receivable	110,000	25,000
Deferred income taxes	173,000	120,000
Change in noncash current assets and liabilities:		
Receivables	(385,000)	(81,000)
Inventories	(834,000)	129,000
Advances on grain purchases and margin deposits	370,000	(87,000)
Prepaid expenses and other current assets	111,000	(58,000)
Accounts payable and accrued expenses	(51,000)	29,000
Salaries, wages, and related payroll taxes	245,000	(146,000)
Net cash provided by operating activities	8,258,000	6,143,000
Cash flows from investing activities:		
Acquisitions of investments and other assets	(457,000)	(175,000)
Acquisitions of property, plant, and other equipment	(4,723,000)	(5,044,000)
Proceeds from sales of property, plant, and equipment	609,000	4,078,000
Net cash used in investing activities	(4,571,000)	(1,141,000)
Cash flows from financing activities:		
Increase in notes payable to bank	611,000	157,000
Repayment of long-term debt	(1,900,000)	(1,175,000)
Patronage refunds and other equity paid in cash	(2,572,000)	(3,811,000)
Proceeds from issuance of common stock	5,000	2,000
Net cash used in financing activities	(3,856,000)	(4,827,000)
Net change in cash and cash equivalents	(169,000)	175,000
Cash and cash equivalents at beginning of year	2,819,000	2,644,000
Cash and cash equivalents at end of year	$ 2,650,000	$ 2,819,000
Supplemental disclosure of cash flow data:		
Cash paid during the years for:		
Interest (net of amounts capitalized)	$ 2,919,000	$ 2,733,000
Income taxes paid	$ 715,000	$ 428,000

The accompanying notes are an integral part of the financial statements.

Central Supply Cooperative
Notes to Financial Statements
Years Ended May 31, 20X2 and 20X1

1. Nature of Operations and Summary of Significant Accounting Policies

Nature of operations. Central Supply Cooperative is an agricultural cooperative association organized to provide a supply source for members and to market farm products delivered by members. The Cooperative's members are located primarily in the Midwestern region of the United States.

Use of estimates. The preparation of financial statements in conformity with generally accepted accounting principles requires management to make estimates and assumptions that affect the reported amounts of assets and liabilities and disclosure of contingent assets and liabilities at the date of the financial statements and the reported amounts of revenues and expenses during the reporting period. Actual results could differ from those estimates.

Cash equivalents. The cooperative considers all highly liquid investments with a maturity of three months or less when purchased to be cash equivalents.

Accounts receivable. Receivables from farm supply and farm marketing sales are based on contracted prices. The cooperative's receivables consist primarily of large groups of smaller-balance homogeneous accounts that are collectively evaluated for impairment. The company provides an allowance for doubtful accounts which is based upon a review of outstanding receivables, historical collection information, and existing economic conditions. Normal trade receivables are due 30 days after the date of sale. Trade receivables past due more than 120 days are considered delinquent. Delinquent receivables are written off based on individual credit evaluation and specific circumstances of the customer.

Inventories. Grain inventories are carried at market.

Sunflower-seed inventory is stated at the lower of cost or market, first-in, first-out method (FIFO).

Supplies and materials are stated at the lower of cost or market, first-in, first-out method (FIFO).

Investments. The investment in Midstate Marketing Cooperative (Midstate) represents equities allocated to the cooperative by Midstate as of Midstate's most recent fiscal year-end, plus an accrual to the cooperative's fiscal year-end for anticipated patronage allocations. The accrual is based on the cooperative's expected percentage (5 percent in both 20X1 and 20X2) of Midstate's total patronage applied to Midstate's interim operating results. Patronage refunds are credited to cost of raw materials, operations, and distribution.

The investment in the Bank for Cooperatives consists of class C stock at cost and the cooperative's share of the bank's allocated surplus. Any patronage refunds received from the bank are credited to interest expense.

The investment in Farm Fertilizers, Inc. (FFI), represents allocated equities for which notification has been received by the cooperative. The patronage earnings of FFI vary substantially from year to year, and FFI does not make interim operating results available to the cooperative. Accordingly, patronage allocations for which notification has not been received cannot be reasonably determined. Patronage refunds are credited to cost of raw materials, operations, and distribution.

Property, plant, and equipment. Property, plant, and equipment are stated at cost. Depreciation is computed principally by using the straight-line method over the estimated useful lives of the related depreciable assets. Expenditures for betterments and renewals that extend useful lives are capitalized. Gains and losses on retirements and disposals are included in net margins.

Long-lived assets. Long-lived assets to be held and used are tested for recoverability whenever events or changes in circumstances indicate that the related carrying amount may not be recoverable. When required, impairment losses on assets to be held and used are recognized based on the fair value of the asset and long-lived assets to be disposed of by sale are reported at the lower of carrying amount or fair value less cost to sell.

Patrons' equities.[*] In accordance with its bylaws, the cooperative allocates patronage margins to its patrons, as determined for income tax purposes, in cash, preferred stock, and certificates of equity in proportions determined by its board of directors.

New members are issued one share of common stock. At any time a member ceases to be active, such shares are redeemed at par value.[**]

Income taxes. The cooperative, as a nonexempt cooperative, is taxed on nonpatronage proceeds and any patronage proceeds not paid or allocated to patrons. Provisions for income taxes are based on taxes payable or refundable for the current year and deferred taxes on temporary differences between the amount of taxable income and pretax financial income and between the tax bases of assets and liabilities and their reported amounts in the financial statements. Deferred tax assets and liabilities are included in the financial statements at currently enacted income tax rates applicable to the period in which the deferred tax assets and liabilities are expected to be realized or settled as prescribed in FASB Statement No. 109, *Accounting for Income Taxes.* As changes in tax laws or rate are enacted, deferred tax assets and liabilities are adjusted through the provision for income taxes.

2. Accounts Receivable

Receivables are composed of the following:

	May 31,	
	20X2	*20X1*
Farm Supply receivables	$3,788,000	$3,798,000
Farm Marketing receivables	3,500,000	3,100,000
Other	35,000	40,000
Less: Allowance for doubtful accounts	(750,000)	(640,000)
	$6,573,000	$6,298,000

3. Inventories

A summary of inventories follows.

	May 31,	
	20X2	*20X1*
Grain	$ 8,211,000	$ 8,105,000
Sunflower seed	3,101,000	3,020,000
Supplies and materials	4,208,000	3,561,000
Total	$15,520,000	$14,686,000

---

[*] See footnote † to the foreword to the Illustrative Financial Statements of Agricultural Cooperatives.

[**] In a situation described above such common stock meets the definition of a mandatorily redeemable financial instrument under FASB Statement No. 150, *Accounting for Certain Financial Instruments With Characteristics of Both Liabilities and Equity,* and as such may have to be reclassified as a liability. See footnote † to the foreword to the Illustrative Financial Statements of Agricultural Cooperatives for the discussion of FASB Statement No. 150.

AAG-APC APP B

Grain purchased from patrons is included as an element of cost of sales, based on the spot-market price of the grain at date of receipt. The value of grain received from patrons amounted to $ 16,427,000 and $ 15,845,000 for the years ended May 31, 20X2 and 20X1, respectively.

4. Notes Payable to Bank and Long-Term Debt

Notes payable to the bank consist of short-term loans from the Bank for Cooperatives. A summary of such borrowings during the years ended May 31, 20X2 and 20X1 follows.

	May 31,	
	20X2	20X1
Borrowings as of May 31	$7,084,000	$6,473,000
Average interest rate on year-end borrowings	15.6%	14.7%
Average borrowings during the year	$8,562,000	$7,679,000
Average interest rate on borrowings during the year	14.9%	14.2%
Maximum borrowings during the year	$9,500,000	$8,650,000

Long-term debt consists of the following:

	May 31,	
	20X2	20X1
Bank for Cooperatives, 12% due in varying installments through 20X9	$6,049,000	$ 6,367,000
Commercial bank loans, at prime, 16% at May 31, 20X2 and 14.5% at May 31, 20X1 due in varying installments through 20X8	3,489,000	5,071,000
	9,538,000	11,438,000
Less current maturities	560,000	1,230,000
Total	$8,978,000	$10,208,000

Aggregate annual principal payments applicable to long-term debt for the five years subsequent to May 31, 20X2 are as follows.

Year Ending May 31,	
20X3	$ 560,000
20X4	601,000
20X5	892,000
20X6	1,802,000
20X7	2,186,000
Thereafter	3,497,000
Total	$9,538,000

Inventories and accounts receivable are pledged as collateral under the short-term agreements with the Bank for Cooperatives. Property, plant, and equipment with book value of $ 12 million, along with the investment in the Bank for Cooperatives, are pledged under the long-term agreements with the Bank for Cooperatives and a commercial bank. The long-term agreements require maintenance of $ 5 million of working capital and agreement with the banks on revolvement of allocated equities and assumption of additional long-term debt.* Additionally, the agreements require the cooperative to invest in class C stock of the Bank for Cooperatives in amounts determined by that bank.

5. Income Taxes

The provision for income taxes consist of the following:

	Years Ended May 31,	
	20X2	20X1
Current		
Federal	$365,000	$305,000
State	112,000	95,000
Total current	477,000	400,000
Deferred		
Federal	139,000	116,000
State	34,000	29,000
Total deferred	173,000	145,000
Total	$650,000	$545,000

The net tax effects of temporary differences between the carrying amounts of assets and liabilities for financial reporting purposes and the amounts used for income tax purposes are reflected in deferred income taxes. Significant components of the company's deferred tax liabilities as of April 30, 20X2 and 20X1 are as follows:

	Years Ended May 31,	
	20X2	20X1
Current deferred tax assets/(liabilities)		
Inventory valuation methods	$ 53,800	$ 47,500
Capitalized costs	(180,000)	(225,000)
Total current deferred tax liability	$ (126,200)	$ (177,500)
Noncurrent deferred tax assets/(liabilities)		
Accelerated depreciation	(1,355,000)	(1,135,000)
Other, (net)	(45,800)	(41,500)
Total noncurrent deferred tax liability	$(1,400,800)	$(1,176,500)

A reconciliation of the income tax provision with amounts determined by applying the federal statutory rate to income taxes is as follows:

	Years Ended May 31,	
	20X2	20X1
Federal statutory income tax rate	34.0%	34.0%
Qualified patronage distributions	(24.2)	(21.7)
State and local income tax	2.3	2.9
Other (net)	(1.7)	(2.3)
Effective tax rate	10.4%	12.9%

---

* FASB Statement No. 150, *Accounting for Certain Financial Instruments With Characteristics of Both Liabilities and Equity*, may have a significant impact on debt covenants by reducing the cooperative's reported capital. See footnote † to the foreword to the Illustrative Financial Statements of Agricultural Cooperatives for the discussion of FASB Statement No. 150.

6. Commitment and Contingencies

The cooperative has signed agreements to purchase machinery and equipment costing approximately $7 million to modernize its grain-handling facilities. These purchases are to be financed by additional long-term debt with the Bank for Cooperatives.

7. Fair Value of Financial Instruments

The carrying amount of the cooperative's current maturities of long-term debt, approximate their fair value. The fair value of net long-term debt, which is based upon borrowing rates currently available to the company for debt issues with similar terms and maturities, is $8,695 (20X1, $9,987).[16, 17]

---

[16] FASB Statement No. 126, *Exemption From Certain Required Disclosures About Financial Instruments for Certain Nonpublic Entities, an Amendment of FASB Statement No. 107,* as amended by FASB Statements No. 133, *Accounting for Derivative Instruments and Hedging Activities,* and No. 149, *Amendment of Statement 133 on Derivative Instruments and Hedging Activities,* amends FASB Statement No. 107, *Disclosures About Fair Value of Financial Instruments,* to make the disclosures about fair value of financial instruments prescribed in FASB Statement No. 107 optional for entities that meet all of the following criteria:

    a. The entity is a nonpublic entity.
    b. The entity's total assets are less than $100 million on the date of the financial statements.
    c. The entity has no instrument that, in whole or in part, is accounted for as a derivative instrument under FASB Statement No. 133, other than commitments related to the origination of mortgage loans to be held for sale, during the reporting period.

[17] SAS No. 101, *Auditing Fair Value Measurements and Disclosures,* contains significantly expanded guidance on the audit procedures for fair value measurements and disclosures. Please refer to paragraphs 12.40–12.43 for a discussion of SAS No. 101.

Appendix C

Statement of Position   85-3

Accounting by Agricultural Producers and Agricultural Cooperatives

April 30, 1985

Issued by
Accounting Standards Division
American Institute of
Certified Public Accountants

NOTICE TO READERS

Statements of Position of the Accounting Standards Division present the conclusions of at least a majority of the Accounting Standards Executive Committee, which is the senior technical body of the AICPA authorized to speak for the Institute in the areas of financial accounting and reporting. Statement on Auditing Standards No. 69, *The Meaning of* Present Fairly in Conformity With Generally Accepted Accounting Principles, identifies AICPA Statements of Position as sources of established accounting principles that an AICPA member should consider if the accounting treatment of a transaction or event is not specified by a pronouncement covered by Rule 203 of the AICPA Code of Professional Conduct. In such circumstances, the accounting treatment specified by this Statement of Position should be used or the member should be prepared to justify a conclusion that another treatment better presents the substance of the transaction in the circumstances. However, an entity need not change an accounting treatment followed as of March 15, 1992 to the accounting treatment specified in this Statement of Position.

TABLE OF CONTENTS

Accounting by Agricultural Producers and Agricultural Cooperatives

Introduction

1. This statement discusses accounting by agricultural producers and agricultural cooperatives that intend to present financial statements in conformity with generally accepted accounting principles. The issues discussed are—

- Accounting for inventories by producers
- Accounting for development costs of land, trees and vines, intermediate-life plants, and animals
- Accounting by patrons for product deliveries to cooperatives
- Accounting by cooperatives for products received from patrons
- Accounting for investments in and income from cooperatives

This statement does not apply to personal financial statements of agricultural producers or statements prepared on a comprehensive basis of accounting other than generally accepted accounting principles, for example, the income tax or the cash basis of accounting. This statement also does not apply to growers of timber; growers of pineapple and sugarcane in tropical regions; raisers of animals for competitive sports; or merchants or noncooperative processors of agricultural products that purchase commodities from growers, contract harvesters, or others serving agricultural producers.

Definitions

2. For purposes of this statement, the following definitions apply.

Advances. Generally used in marketing and pooling cooperatives to denote amounts paid to patrons prior to final settlement; for example, amounts paid to patrons on delivery of crops.

Agricultural cooperatives. See paragraphs 6 through 22.

Agricultural producers. See paragraphs 3 through 5.

Assigned amounts. Amounts used to record products delivered by patrons of a marketing cooperative operating on a pooling basis, and the related liability to patrons if the ultimate amounts to be paid to patrons are determined when the pool is closed. These amounts may be established on the basis of current prices paid by other buyers (sometimes referred to as "field prices"), or they may be established by the cooperative's board of directors. The assigned amounts are sometimes referred to as "established values."

Cash advance method. A method of accounting for inventories of a marketing cooperative operating on a pooling basis. Under this method, inventories are accounted for at the amount of cash advances made to patrons. (This is sometimes referred to as the "cost advance method.")

Commercial production. The point at which production from an orchard, vineyard, or grove first reaches a level that makes operations economically feasible, based on prices normally expected to prevail.

Crop development costs. Costs incurred up to the time crops are produced in commercial quantities, including the costs of land preparation, plants, planting, fertilization, grafting, pruning, equipment use, and irrigation.

Crops. Grains, vegetables, fruits, berries, nuts, and fibers grown by agricultural producers.

Exempt and nonexempt cooperatives.   Cooperatives classified according to their federal income tax status. Both types are permitted to deduct from taxable income patronage distributed or allocated on a qualified basis to patrons to the extent that the distributions represent earnings of the cooperative derived from business done with or for the patrons. In addition, cooperatives meeting the requirements of Internal Revenue Code section 521 (exempt cooperatives) are permitted to deduct (1) limited amounts paid as dividends on capital stock and (2) distributions to patrons of income from business done with the U.S. government or its agencies and income from nonpatronage sources.

Farm price method.   A method of accounting for inventories at the sales prices in the nearest local market for the quantities that the producer normally sells less the estimated costs of disposition.

Futures contract.   A standard and transferable form of contract that binds the seller to deliver to the bearer a standard amount and grade of a commodity to a specific location at a specified time. It usually includes a schedule of premiums and discounts for quality variation.

Growing crop.   A field, row, tree, bush, or vine crop before harvest.

Grove.   Fruit or nut trees planted in geometric patterns to economically facilitate care of the trees and harvest of the fruit or nuts.

Harvested crop.   An agricultural product, gathered but unsold.

Livestock.   Registered and commercial cattle, sheep, hogs, horses, poultry, and small animals bred and raised by agricultural producers.

Market order prices.   Prices for raw products established by federal or state agencies.

Marketing cooperative.   A cooperative that markets the products (crops, livestock, and so on) produced by its patrons.

Member and nonmember (of a cooperative).   A member is an owner-patron who is entitled to vote at corporate meetings of a cooperative. A nonmember patron is not entitled to voting privileges. A nonmember patron may or may not be entitled to share in patronage distributions, depending on the articles and bylaws of the cooperative or on other agreements.

Net realizable value.   Valuation of inventories at estimated selling prices in the ordinary course of business, less reasonably predictable costs of completion, disposal, and transportation.

Orchard.   Fruit trees planted in geometric patterns to economically facilitate care of the trees and harvest of the fruit.

Patron.   Any individual, trust, estate, partnership, corporation, or cooperative with or for whom a cooperative does business on a cooperative basis, whether a member or nonmember of the cooperative association.

Patronage.   The amount of business done with a cooperative by one of its patrons. Patronage is measured by either the quantity or value of commodities received from patrons by a marketing cooperative and the quantity or value of the goods and services sold to patrons by a supply cooperative.

Patronage allocations.   Patronage earnings distributed, or allocated, to individual patrons on the basis of each patron's proportionate share of total patronage. Such allocations, which include notification to the patron, may be made on a qualified or nonqualified basis.

Patronage earnings. The excess of a cooperative's revenues over its costs arising from transactions done with or for its patrons. Generally a significant portion of those earnings is allocated to the cooperative's patrons in the form of cash, allocated equities, or both.

Pools. Accounting control centers used for determining earnings and patronage refunds due to particular patrons.

> Open pools are accounting control centers that are not closed at the end of each accounting period. Open pools are sometimes used by marketing cooperatives for crops that may not be sold for two or more years after their receipt from patrons.

> A single pool cooperative determines net proceeds or patronage refunds on the basis of overall operating results for all commodities marketed during an accounting period.

> A multiple pool cooperative determines net proceeds or patronage refunds on the basis of separate commodities, departments, or accounting periods.

Progeny. Offspring of animals or plants.

Raised animals. Animals produced and raised from an owned herd, as opposed to purchased animals.

Recurring land development costs. Costs that do not result in permanent or long-term improvements to land, for example, maintenance costs that occur annually or periodically.

Retains. Amounts determined on a per-unit basis or as a percentage of patronage earnings that are withheld by cooperatives from distributions and allocated to patrons' capital accounts.

Supply cooperative. A cooperative that supplies to its patrons goods and services used by them in producing their products.

Unit livestock method. Accounting for livestock by using an arbitrary fixed periodic charge. For raised animals the amount is accumulated by periodic increments from birth to maturity or disposition. For purchased animals the arbitrary fixed periodic amount is added to the acquisition cost until maturity or disposition of the animal.

Vineyards. Grapevines planted in patterns for commercial cultivation and production.

Written notice of allocation. Any capital stock, revolving fund certificate, retain certificate, certificate of indebtedness, letter of advice, or other written notice to the recipient that states the dollar amount allocated to the patron by the cooperative and the portion that constitutes a patronage dividend.

Agricultural Producers

3. In this statement, farmers and ranchers are referred to as "agricultural producers," a term that includes, for example, those who raise crops from seeds or seedlings, breed livestock (whether registered or commercial), and feed livestock in preparation for slaughter. The term excludes, for example, merchants and processors of agricultural products who purchase commodities from growers, contract harvesters, or others serving agricultural producers, although they are covered by the term "agribusiness" as it is generally used. The term also excludes growers of timber and raisers of animals for competitive sports, although some of the accounting principles discussed in this statement may apply to such activities.

4. Agricultural producers use every form of business organization, from sole proprietorship to large publicly held corporation. They engage in numerous activities, for example:

- Growing wheat, milo, corn, and other grains
- Growing soybeans, vegetables, sugar beets, and sugarcane
- Growing citrus fruits, other fruits, grapes, berries, and nuts
- Growing cotton and other vegetable fibers
- Operating plant nurseries
- Breeding and feeding cattle, hogs, and sheep, including animals for wool production
- Operating dairies
- Operating poultry and egg production facilities
- Breeding horses
- Raising mink, chinchilla, and similar small animals

In addition, the operations of agricultural producers often involve various combinations of those activities. Agricultural practices and products may vary still further because of differences in temperature, soil, rainfall, and regional economics. Farm products may be used in related activities, such as the feeding of hay and grain to livestock, or they may be marketed directly by the producer. Producers often sell products in accordance with government programs or through agricultural cooperatives. Marketing strategies may include forward contracts or commodity futures contracts to reduce the risks of fluctuations in market prices.

5. Agricultural producers often borrow to finance crop development costs and the costs of acquiring facilities and equipment.

Agricultural Cooperatives

[6.—8.] [Deleted to remove outdated information.]

9. Section 1141(j) of the Agricultural Marketing Act of 1929, as amended, contains the following definition of a cooperative association:

The term "cooperative association" means any association in which farmers act together in processing, preparing for market, handling, and/or marketing the farm products of persons so engaged, and also means any association in which farmers act together in purchasing, testing, grading, processing, distributing, and/or furnishing farm supplies and/or farm business services. Provided, however, that such associations are operated for producers or purchasers and conform to one or both of the following requirements:

First. That no member of the association is allowed more than one vote because of the amount of stock or membership capital he may own therein; and

Second. That the association does not pay dividends on stock or membership capital in excess of 8 per centum per annum.

And in any case to the following:

Third. That the association shall not deal in farm products, farm supplies, and farm business services with or for nonmembers in an amount greater in value that the total amount of such business transacted by it with or for members. All business transacted by any cooperative association for or on behalf of the United States or any agency or instrumentality thereof shall be disregarded in determining the volume of member and nonmember business transacted by such association.

10. A cooperative typically has the following characteristics:

a. Assets are distributed periodically to patrons on a patronage basis. In certain situations, however, assets in the amount of net-of-tax earnings may be accumulated by the cooperative and may or may not be allocated to patrons' accounts.

b. Members control the organization in their capacity as patrons and not as equity investors.

c. Membership is limited to patrons.

d. The return that can be paid on capital investment is limited.

e. At least 50 percent of the cooperative's business is done on a patronage basis.

11. Virtually all agricultural cooperatives meet the definition of cooperatives that is used to determine eligibility for borrowing from the banks for cooperatives and for exemption from the annual reporting requirements of the Securities and Exchange Act of 1934. Failure to meet the definition, however, does not necessarily prevent an entity from being considered as operating on a cooperative basis under subchapter T of the Internal Revenue Code.

12. The main difference between cooperatives and other business enterprises is that cooperatives and their patrons operate as single economic units to accomplish specific business purposes, such as the marketing of farm products, the purchase of supplies, or the performance of services for the benefit of the patrons. The aim is to reduce costs, increase sales proceeds, and share risks through the increased bargaining power that results from the patrons' combined resources and buying power.

13. The patron's role as an investor is secondary and incidental to his business relationship with the cooperative.

14. If certain requirements are met, the Internal Revenue Code permits cooperatives tax deductions for earnings allocated to their patrons. Earnings not so allocated are taxed at corporate income tax rates. Cooperatives may use other terms for earnings, such as "margins," "net proceeds," or "savings."

15. Another difference between cooperatives and other business corporations is that the cooperative's bylaws usually require it to distribute assets to patrons, or allocate to patrons' accounts amounts equal to its earnings, on the basis of their patronage. Distributions to patrons are different from dividend payments to stockholders in other corporations. The distribution of earnings on the basis of patronage has been termed the "price adjustment theory."

16. Under the price adjustment theory, a cooperative agrees to do business at cost. In a purchasing cooperative, for example, a patron may be charged more than cost at the time of purchase; however, the cooperative normally must return to the patron all amounts received in excess of cost, including costs of operation and processing.

17. Both exempt and nonexempt cooperatives are subject to federal income taxes on patronage earnings that are not distributed in cash or allocated on a qualified basis. Nonexempt cooperatives are subject to income taxes on earnings arising from sources other than patronage.

18. Cooperatives generally try to buy or sell at the current market price. Periodically, they determine total costs and make distributions to patrons in the form of cash, certificates, or other notices of allocation based on the excess of revenues over costs.

19. The two major types of cooperatives are supply cooperatives and marketing cooperatives. *Supply cooperatives* obtain or produce such items as building materials, equipment, feed, seeds, fertilizer, and petroleum products for their patrons. *Marketing cooperatives* provide means for agricultural producers to process and sell their products.

20. Services related to those functions are provided by some supply and marketing cooperatives; they are also provided by separate associations known as *service cooperatives,* which provide such services as trucking, storage, accounting, and data processing. A special type of service cooperative is a *bargaining cooperative,* which serves its members by negotiating with processors on their behalf.

21. Many marketing cooperatives commingle patrons' fungible products in pools. The excess of revenues over costs for each pool is allocated to patrons on the basis of their pro rata contributions to the pool, which may be determined by the number of units delivered, the volume of product delivered, or another equitable method.

22. The members of *local cooperatives* are agricultural producers whose activities are generally centralized. The members of *federated cooperatives* are other cooperatives whose activities are regional. Some cooperatives have both individual producers and other cooperatives as members.

Accounting for Inventories of Crops by Agricultural Producers

23. Previously existing accounting literature does not specifically cover accounting by agricultural producers, and available material is predominantly tax oriented. Accounting Research Bulletin (ARB) No. 43, chapter 4, provides the following information about accounting for inventories:

STATEMENT 9

Only in exceptional cases may inventories properly be stated above cost. For example, precious metals having a fixed monetary value with no substantial cost of marketing may be stated at such monetary value; any other exceptions must be justifiable by inability to determine appropriate approximate costs, immediate marketability at quoted market price, and the characteristic of unit interchangeability. Where goods are stated above cost this fact should be fully disclosed.

Discussion

It is generally recognized that income accrues only at the time of sale, and that gains may not be anticipated by reflecting assets at their current sales prices. For certain articles, however, exceptions are permissible. Inventories of gold and silver, when there is an effective government-controlled market at a fixed monetary value, are ordinarily reflected at selling prices. A similar treatment is not uncommon for inventories representing agricultural, mineral, and other products, units of which are interchangeable and have an immediate marketability at quoted prices and for which appropriate costs may be difficult to obtain. Where such inventories are stated at sales prices, they should of course be reduced by expenditures to be incurred in disposal, and the use of such basis should be fully disclosed in the financial statements.

24. Accounting Principles Board (APB) Statement No. 4, chapter 6, paragraph 16, states the following:

Revenue is sometimes recognized on bases other than the realization rule. For example, on long-term construction contracts revenue may be recognized as construction progresses. This exception to the realization principle is based on the availability of evidence of the ultimate proceeds and the consensus that a better measure of periodic income results. Sometimes revenue is recognized at the completion of production and before a sale is made. Examples include certain precious metals and farm products with assured sales prices. The assured price, the difficulty in some situations of determining costs of products on hand, and the characteristic of unit interchangeability are reasons given to support this exception.

Statement of Position 93-3, *Rescission of Accounting Principles Board Statements*, rescinds APB Statement No. 4. FASB Concepts Statement No. 5, *Recognition and Measurement in Financial Statements of Business Enterprises*, discusses matters similar to those in APB Statement No. 4.

25. Accounting Research Study (ARS) 13, chapter 9, page 156, states—

Market as the Accounting Basis of Inventories

Exceptional cases exist in which it is not practicable to determine an appropriate cost basis for products. A market basis is acceptable if the products (1) have immediate marketability at quoted market prices that cannot be influenced by the producer, (2) have characteristics of unit interchangeability, and (3) have relatively insignificant costs of disposal. The accounting basis of those kinds of inventories should be their realizable value, calculated on the basis of quoted market prices less estimated direct costs of disposal. Examples are precious metals produced as joint products or by-products of extractive processes and fresh dressed meats produced in meat packing operations.

Paragraph 67 of FASB Concepts Statement No. 5 also discusses measurement of assets at current market value.

Diversity in Practice

26. Published financial statements reveal several ways that agricultural producers account for growing crops:

- Charging costs to operations when they are incurred
- Including crop development costs in deferred charges and amortizing them
- Stating costs on the balance sheet at unchanging amounts substantially less than the costs incurred and charging all current costs to operations when they are incurred
- Deferring all costs and writing them off at harvest or, for perennial crops, over the estimated productive life of the planting

    Agricultural producers report harvested crops using the farm price method, at cost (LIFO, FIFO, or average cost), and at the lower of cost or market.

Some producers use the farm price method (market) to account for inventories of harvested crops. Other agricultural producers, particularly those whose securities are publicly held, account for harvested crops at the lower of cost or market.

Pros and Cons

27. A study of accounting for producers' inventories involves an examination of chapter 4, statement 9, of ARB No. 43, which has been used as authority for accounting for producers' inventories at market.

28. Some accountants believe that many producers cannot determine costs, and some believe that market is an appropriate valuation, whether or not cost data are available. Many accountants believe that users of producers' financial statements would find them less useful if inventories were valued at the lower of cost or market.

29. Other reasons for the preference for market value are its long established use and the need to identify separately the gains and losses attributable to the production cycle and the marketing function, which is discussed in paragraph 35.

30. For most business activities, the accounting literature requires an exchange of goods or services before income is recognized. That precludes accounting for inventories of unsold goods at market unless market value is less than cost. The principal exceptions to that rule are identified in chapter 9 of ARS 13 as "metals produced as joint products or by-products of extractive processes and fresh dressed meats produced in meat packing operations." Those products have unique cost identification problems. Chapter 9 of ARS 13 further states that carrying products at market is acceptable if those products "(1) have immediate marketability at quoted market prices that cannot be influenced by the producer, (2) have characteristics of unit interchangeability, and (3) have relatively insignificant costs of disposal."

31. The first of the three conditions in ARB No. 43, statement 9, is the inability to determine costs. While many producers may not keep detailed cost records, costs usually either are available or can be determined with acceptable accuracy.

32. Accountants who favor accounting for producers' inventories at market recognize that ARB No. 43 requires an *inability* to determine appropriate approximate costs. They point out, however, that the discussion interprets the statement to apply when "appropriate costs may be *difficult* to obtain" [emphasis added]. They also note that APB Statement 4,[*] chapter 6, referred to the "difficulty in some situations of determining costs of products" as a partial justification for the use of market price. Thus, they interpret statement 9 as allowing the use of market if costs are difficult to determine, not only if they are impossible to determine.

33. A major argument for accounting for inventories at market is the availability of established markets that provide quoted market prices for most agricultural commodities. However, because variations in grade and quantity, distance from central markets, shipping hazards, and other restrictions may affect the ultimate realization of quoted market prices for agricultural products, there are often serious difficulties in determining the market price for a given product in a given place. Also, many products have no central market with established prices, and determination of their market prices may be subjective and incapable of verification.

34. While ARS 13 does not cover inventories of agricultural products, it questions the appropriateness of accounting for inventories at market even if an established market exists. The study notes that present principles appear to allow the use of market price in accounting for inventories of precious metals if there is a fixed selling price and insignificant marketing cost regardless of whether it is practicable to determine costs. The study states—

> The apparent preferential treatment may have originally been considered appropriate because metals having fixed monetary values clearly demonstrated the "immediate marketability at quoted market prices and the characteristic of interchangeability" required in the cases in which it is impracticable to determine costs. Further question as to why preferential treatment was originally accorded to precious metals might now be considered academic.

---

[*] Statement of Position 93-3, *Rescission of Accounting Principles Board Statements*, rescinds APB Statement No. 4.

Silver no longer has a fixed monetary price, and gold has a fluctuating free market price for nonmonetary purposes. That raises questions as to whether the inventory basis for gold and silver should now be considered the same as for other metals produced as by-products or joint products.

35. Some proponents of accounting for agricultural producers' inventories at market distinguish the production of a crop from its marketing; they believe that delays in the disposal of a harvested crop are due principally to the producer's desire to sell the commodities later at a higher price. They contend that, in order to separate the results of the two functions, the inventories should be accounted for at market prices after they are harvested. They point out that both functions are likely to cause significant gains and losses. Some opponents counter that the same argument can be made for many nonagricultural enterprises that are not permitted to recognize income at the end of production.

36. The securities of most agricultural producers are not traded publicly, and their financial statements are prepared primarily for management and lenders. Advocates of the use of market prices contend that lenders are concerned with the market price of inventories to be used as collateral. Moreover, most producers are not required to use cost information for income tax purposes. Thus, some accountants argue that determining cost for financial statements is an unproductive additional burden to the producer. Conversely, cost advocates point out that both public and nonpublic producers require long-term financing, and cost-basis financial statements may provide better information for those purposes.

37. Some accountants believe that it is difficult to argue persuasively for charging the periodic costs of growing crops to expense as they are incurred since a valuable asset is being developed. Some contend that the use of a fixed amount less than cost violates existing principles of accounting for assets. Others believe it is acceptable and consistent with a market basis of accounting to account for growing crops at net realizable value or at no value.

Division Conclusions

38. All direct and indirect costs of growing crops should be accumulated and growing crops should be reported at the lower of cost or market.

39. An agricultural producer should report inventories of harvested crops held for sale at (a) the lower of cost or market or (b) in accordance with established industry practice, at sales price less estimated costs of disposal, when all the following conditions exist:

- The product has a reliable, readily determinable and realizable market price.
- The product has relatively insignificant and predictable costs of disposal.
- The product is available for immediate delivery.

Accounting for Development Costs of Land, Trees and Vines, Intermediate-Life Plants, and Animals

40. Development costs of land, trees and vines, intermediate-life plants, and animals are different from costs incurred in raising crops for harvest, which were discussed in the previous section, "Accounting for Inventories of Crops by Agricultural Producers."

41. Land development generally includes improvements to bring the land into a suitable condition for general agricultural use and to maintain its productive condition. Some improvements are permanent; some have a limited life. Permanent land developments include, for example, clearing, initial level-ing, terracing, and construction of earthen dams; they involve changes to the grade and contour of the ground and generally have an indefinite life if they are properly maintained. Limited-life developments usually include such items as water distribution systems and fencing and may also include the costs of wells, levees, ponds, drain tile, and ditches, depending on the climate, topogra-phy, soil conditions, and farming practices in the area.

42. Orchards, vineyards, and groves generally develop over several years before they reach commercial production. Production continues for varying numbers of years, depending on such influences as type of plant, soil, and climate. During development, the plants normally require grafting, pruning, spraying, cultivation, or other care.

43. Intermediate-life plants have growth and production cycles of more than one year but less than those of trees and vines. They include, for example, artichokes, various types of berries, asparagus, alfalfa, and grazing grasses. Development costs of intermediate-life plants include the cost of land prepara-tion, plants, and cultural care until the plant, bush, or vine begins to produce in commercial quantities.

44. The terms *livestock* and *animals* are used interchangeably and are meant to include cattle, sheep, hogs, horses, poultry, and other small animals. The development of animals requires care and maintenance of the breeding stock and their progeny until their transfer from the brood herd. Animals purchased before maturity also require care and maintenance to ready them for productive use or sale. The animals are ultimately identified for transfer to breeding herds, dairy herds, or other productive functions, are selected for sale, or are transferred to a feeding or other marketing operation.

Diversity in Practice

45. Development costs of land, trees and vines, intermediate-life plants, and animals are accounted for in the following ways:
- Charged to operations when they are incurred
- Included in deferred charges
- Included on the balance sheet at fixed amounts substantially less than the costs incurred, with all or a majority of the current costs charged to operations as they are incurred
- Capitalized and amortized over the estimated productive life of the animal, tree, vine, or plant
- Carried at market values

46. In the case of annual field crops that are planted and harvested in the same accounting period, producers generally match costs with revenues. When the growing cycle continues beyond the accounting period, costs often are not matched with revenues.

47. Few significant diversities of practice are apparent in the financial statements primarily because of lack of disclosure. However, some agricultural producers charge land development costs to expense based on provisions of the income tax laws.

48. In accounting for development costs of trees and vines, some produc-ers agree that the costs should be capitalized and depreciated over the expected productive life, but the costs to be capitalized and those to be charged to expense are not identified uniformly. Income tax concepts have had a strong influence on accounting practices for those development costs.

49. Crops from intermediate-life plants have generally been accounted for in the same way as annual crops, with no distinctions for variations in the periods of development and productivity.

50. Many livestock producers charge the costs of developing animals to expense without regard to their productive lives or future use or sales value. Animals are sometimes reported at cost and other times at market values. Some producers use the unit livestock method, and in many instances, the annual unit cost increments are below market and probably below cost.

Pros and Cons

51. Some accountants believe that large-scale improvements that transform the land to new and better uses are permanent land improvements to be capitalized and that subsequent modifications and improvements are necessary and should be classified as period expenses.

52. Others believe that it is difficult, or nearly impossible, to distinguish between permanent, limited-life, and recurring land development costs. Land improvements that an owner has made over many years tend to lose their original characteristics. Such improvements are usually accompanied by increasingly intensive land use over relatively long periods. Prior improvements are modified, improved on, or eliminated, and the resulting land configuration and use are noticeably changed. The characteristics of continuing land improvements accomplished over long periods are given as justification for classifying those costs as recurring.

53. Many accountants believe that all direct and related indirect costs of land development, such as leveling, clearing of brush, terracing, and installation of drain tile, should be capitalized. They further believe that land development costs that waste away or diminish in efficiency through use, such as drainage tile, should be depreciated or amortized over the number of seasons that the land can reasonably be expected to produce without renovation or renewal of the particular development.

54. It is generally agreed that development costs of orchards, vineyards, and groves should be capitalized, but there is no agreement on the specific costs that should be capitalized. Many believe it necessary to capitalize only those costs that the income tax laws require to be capitalized.

55. Some accountants believe that all direct and indirect costs for orchards, vineyards, and groves incurred during the development period should be capitalized until commercial production is achieved. Others believe all such costs, except annual maintenance costs, should be capitalized. All agree that capitalized costs should be depreciated or amortized over the useful life of the plantings.

56. Accounting practices for development costs of intermediate-life plants are inconsistent. Producers who deduct expenses before revenues are realized for intermediate-life plants and orchardists and vineyardists who do not want to capitalize development costs and depreciate them over the estimated productive life of the developed asset are motivated by the same reasons. The question of capitalization and depreciation is similar for producers of intermediate-life plants and for producers of trees and vines. The principal distinctions are in development period and productive life. For example, orchard trees may require four to seven years before nominal production, while limited production may occur during the first year of such crops as alfalfa, some berries, and asparagus.

57. Some accountants have resisted accumulating development costs for growing animals, based on the difficulty and expense of accumulating such information and, in some instances, the problem of identifying individual animals or groups and categories of animals. Instead of cost, the unit livestock

method or a market value has been used for assigning amounts to the animals at each level of maturity in the belief that such accounting methods, if consistently applied, would not adversely affect income recognition.

58. Others believe that all direct and indirect development costs of raising livestock should be accumulated and capitalized until the livestock have reached maturity and have been selected for breeding or other productive purposes. Many believe that income-producing livestock should be depreciated on the basis of their expected productive lives.

Division Conclusions*

59. Permanent land development costs should be capitalized and should not be depreciated or amortized, since they have, by definition, an indefinite useful life.

60. Limited-life land development costs and direct and indirect development costs of orchards, groves, vineyards, and intermediate-life plants should be capitalized during the development period and depreciated over the estimated useful life of the land development or that of the tree, vine or plant.

61. All direct and indirect costs of developing animals should be accumulated until the animals reach maturity and are transferred to a productive function. At that point the accumulated development costs, less any estimated salvage value, should be depreciated over the animals' estimated productive lives.

62. All direct and indirect development costs of animals raised for sale should be accumulated, and the animals should be accounted for at the lower of cost or market until they are available for sale. Agricultural producers should report animals available and held for sale (a) at the lower of cost or market or (b) in accordance with established industry practice at sales price, less estimated costs of disposal, when all of the following conditions exist:

- There are reliable, readily determinable and realizable market prices for the animals.
- The costs of disposal are relatively insignificant and predictable.
- The animals are available for immediate delivery.

Accounting for Patrons' Product Deliveries to Marketing Cooperatives Operating on a Pooling Basis

63. Agricultural marketing cooperatives process and market their patrons' products. There are frequently good bases for recording transfers of products between cooperatives and their patrons. For example, dairy cooperatives record transfers of products on the basis of market order prices, and grain cooperatives record transfers of products on the basis of readily determined cash prices. Many cooperatives, therefore, transfer patrons' products at market prices, and the transactions are treated as purchases by the cooperatives and as sales by the patrons.

---

* In July 2001, AcSEC issued an exposure draft of a proposed SOP, *Accounting for Certain Costs and Activities Related to Property, Plant, and Equipment*. Concurrently, the FASB issued an exposure draft of a proposed Statement of Financial Accounting Standards, *Accounting in Interim and Annual Financial Statements for Certain Costs and Activities Related to Property, Plant, and Equipment, an amendment of APB Opinions No. 20 and 28 and FASB Statements No. 51 and 67 and a rescission of FASB Statement No. 73*. That proposed Statement includes amendments to certain FASB pronouncements that would be made in conjunction with issuance of the proposed SOP.

The proposed SOP may amend the presentation and disclosure requirements with respect to property, plant and equipment. A final pronouncement is expected to be issued in the fourth quarter of 2003. Readers should be alert to any final pronouncement.

64. However, cooperatives operating on a pooling basis may receive products from their patrons without paying a fixed price to the patrons. A cooperative may assign amounts to products based on current prices paid by other buyers or on amounts established by the cooperative's board of directors, or it may assign no amount. The cooperative estimates a liability to patrons equal to the assigned amount for the delivered product, and it usually pays this liability on a short-term basis. The excess of revenues over the assigned amounts and operating costs at the end of a pool period, which may be a week, a month, a year, or longer, is paid or allocated to patrons. Assets equal to that excess may be distributed to the patrons or retained by the cooperative.

65. The different accounting methods used by pooling cooperatives have been developed to satisfy provisions of their bylaws and contractual arrangements with patrons and to provide equitable methods of settlement from pool period to pool period, as well as among the various classes of patrons. For pooling cooperatives, accounting methods have been developed to allow the use of the single-pool or multiple-pool methods of accounting.

Diversity in Practice

66. Significant information about the accounting practices of patrons in recording the delivery of raw products to marketing cooperatives is scarce. Among the practices used are recognition (1) at the estimated net return, presumably at the time of delivery, and (2) at the time of sale by the cooperative to an outside party. Those two examples provide the extremes, one recognizing the delivery to the cooperative as a sale and the other continuing to carry the product as inventory of the producer until it is sold by the cooperative. Transfer prices for products delivered to cooperatives are established in diverse ways:

- At market order price or governmental support price
- At market price
- At an assigned amount determined by the cooperative's board of directors to approximate market price
- At the amount of advances
- At cost to the producer
- At no amount until the cooperative advises the producer of the expected proceeds from the ultimate disposition of the product

67. Cooperatives that receive products from patrons and pay their patrons a firm market price, at or shortly after delivery, treat the payments as purchases. In those situations the prices are paid regardless of the amount of the cooperatives' earnings. Those cooperatives normally report inventories at the lower of cost or market. However, pooling cooperatives estimate amounts due to patrons at the time of delivery, and those amounts are later adjusted on the basis of the pool's earnings. This presents a significant accounting problem. The following paragraphs discuss only the accounting issues that result from deliveries of products by patrons to cooperatives operating on a pooling basis.

68. In cooperatives operating on a pooling basis, products delivered by patrons are commingled with other patrons' products, processed, and marketed. Earnings from the sale of finished products are returned to patrons, either in cash or in some form of equity, whether or not those earnings were determined on the basis of current market prices at the time of delivery. Many cooperatives value patrons' products at assigned amounts (usually current market prices) set by the board of directors at delivery. A corresponding estimated liability is accrued for amounts due to patrons. At the end of the pool period, the pool's net earnings are credited to amounts due patrons on a patronage basis.

69. Some cooperatives cannot determine the market prices of patrons' products when they receive them because of limited cash purchases by other processors. They are usually cooperatives that process and market a high percentage of limited specialty crops. Many of those cooperatives account for inventories of goods in process and finished goods at net realizable value, determined by deducting estimated completion and disposition costs from the estimated sales value of the processed inventory, because a reliable price for the unprocessed product is not available to account for inventories at the lower of cost or market. Furthermore, many cooperatives must determine net realizable value to comply with bylaw provisions and contractual obligations and to facilitate equitable pool settlements from pool period to pool period and among various classes of patrons.

70. A 1973 survey by the National Council of Farmer Cooperatives indicated that many marketing cooperatives use net realizable value to account for inventories. An excerpt from an article on this subject prepared for the council's legal, tax, and accounting committee appears below.

The National Council of Farmer Cooperatives made a survey of the inventory valuation methods used by its marketing cooperatives. The results of this survey confirm what has been the private belief of most cooperative accountants, that the net realizable market value method is perhaps the most widely used and accepted method of inventory valuation by marketing cooperatives. This survey reflects the responses of 49 cooperatives and, in summary, indicates that the following inventory methods are in use.

Method	Cooper-atives	Sales (In Thousands)	% of Total Sales
Net realizable market value	24	$2,310,938	48%
Lower of cost or market, using field price as the established value of raw product	8	630,898	13
Net realizable market value and lower of cost or market, using field price as the established value of raw product	5	802,867	17
Cost	2	53,400	1
Rev. Rul. 69-67[*]	7	367,469	8
Other	3	621,925	13
	49	$4,787,497	100%

[*] Note: Rev. Rul 69-67 refers to the cash advance method.

71. The net realizable value method of accounting for inventories permits the recognition of the pool's estimated net earnings at the end of the fiscal period in which the patrons supply their crops to the cooperative or when pools are closed. Inventories are stated at net realizable value, and the amounts due to patrons are credited with the earnings. The net realizable value method of accounting for inventories permits the closing of the pools and provides equitable treatment to patrons if the cooperative transfers the inventories forward to the next period's pool at estimated market value.

72. Some marketing cooperatives receive products from patrons without assigning amounts to them. During the year, cash is advanced to patrons on the basis of anticipated earnings. Inventories are recorded at amounts advanced plus costs of processing, and patrons' products are valued at the amount of advances made to the date of the financial statements. This is commonly called the "cash advance method."

Authoritative Literature

73. The primary source of authoritative guidance for accounting for inventories that result from deliveries of products by patrons to cooperatives has been ARB No. 43.

Pros and Cons

74. A transaction is usually completed when a patron delivers his product to a cooperative. The patron's product is commingled with that of other patrons, and title and individual risk of loss have passed. Some accountants believe that no accounting is necessary at the time of delivery because the transfer price is frequently not known until some later date. Nevertheless, accrual basis accounting calls for reporting the transaction according to the best information available at the time. While greater accuracy may be achieved by waiting for the cooperative to advise the patron of the net proceeds, the handicap of not having current financial information could outweigh the benefit of greater accuracy, and the lack of consistency in reporting could be confusing to the users of the financial statements.

75. Some accountants argue that pooling cooperatives should not use an assigned amount for products received from patrons for financial accounting and reporting purposes because the amounts may not be reliable and the patrons may be paid more or less than that amount at the end of the pool period. Others argue that the use of an assigned amount permits the establishment of a tentative liability due patrons and allows inventories to be stated at the lower of cost or market. The method also facilitates allocation of pool proceeds to patrons.

76. Some accountants believe that the net realizable value method of accounting for inventories is unacceptable because it anticipates cooperative earnings. Further, they believe that future selling prices and disposition costs are too uncertain to base accounting on them. Alternatively, those who favor the use of the net realizable value method believe that the problems of determining net realizable value do not differ from those of determining market under the lower of cost or market method. They also consider the method to be acceptable in accounting for pools because it enables the cooperative to settle pools annually and to comply with bylaw provisions and contractual obligations. In essence, they claim, the inventory is transferred to the next period's pool on an equitable basis.

77. Some accountants believe that cooperatives may record products received from patrons at assigned amounts and then account for the inventories at net realizable value. That method permits the closing of pools at least annually on an equitable basis. Others believe that if assigned amounts are used on receipt of the product, the inventories should be accounted for at the lower of cost or market.

78. Some accountants favor the cash advance method of accounting for inventories. They believe that the only product cost that should be accounted for is the total of cash advanced to patrons to the date of the financial statements, because the cooperative has no liability to pay more unless more is earned. Others favor the cash advance method because the Internal Revenue Service has held in several rulings that pooling cooperatives should use that method in tax computations. Others reject the cash advance method because advances to patrons are primarily determined on availability of cash, the percentage of the pool production sold to the date of the financial statements, and short-term inventory loan restrictions rather than on the value of products received. Further, they reject the method because the amount and timing of advances are generally subject to the board of directors' action and may vary from period to period.

Division Conclusions

Accounting by Patrons for Products Delivered to Pooling Cooperatives

79. If control over the future economic benefits relating to the product has passed, which ordinarily is evidenced by the transfer of title, and if a price is available by reference to contemporaneous transactions in the market, or if the cooperative establishes an assigned amount, a delivery to the cooperative should be recorded as a sale by the patron at that amount on the date of delivery. If there is a reasonable indication that the proceeds from the cooperative will be less than the market price or the assigned amount, the lower amount should be used.

80. If control over the future economic benefits relating to the product has passed, which ordinarily is evidenced by the transfer of title, and there are neither prices determined by other market buyers nor amounts assigned by the cooperative, or if such amounts are erratic, unstable, or volatile, the patron should record the delivery to the cooperative as a sale at the recorded amount of the inventory and should record an unbilled receivable. If there is a reasonable indication that the proceeds from the cooperative will be less than the receivable, the lower amount should be used.

81. If title has not passed, the identity of the individual patron's product is maintained by the cooperative, and the price to the patron is to be based on the identified product's sale, the transaction is not complete, and the product should be included in the patron's inventory until it is sold by the cooperative, at which time the patron should record the sale.

82. Advances are financing devices and should be treated as reductions in the unbilled receivable and should not be used as amounts for recording sales.

Accounting by Pooling Cooperatives for Products Received From Patrons

83. If the boards of directors of agricultural marketing cooperatives operating on a pooling basis with no obligation to pay patrons fixed prices (pooling cooperatives) assign amounts that approximate estimated market to unprocessed products received from patrons, the assigned amounts are cost and should be charged to cost of goods sold and credited to amounts due patrons. The inventories should be accounted for at the lower of cost or market or, as described more fully in paragraph 84, at net realizable value. When assigned amounts are used, they should approximate estimated market of unprocessed products delivered by patrons (an example of inventories at lower of cost or market is provided in the appendix, column A). The method used and the dollar amounts assigned to members' products should be disclosed.

84. If the boards of directors of pooling cooperatives assign amounts to products received from patrons, the cooperatives should use those assigned amounts in determining the estimated amounts due patrons. Such cooperatives may use net realizable value for determining pool proceeds, transferring inventory amounts to subsequent pools, or for other purposes (an example is provided in the appendix, column B). The method used and the dollar amounts assigned to members' products should be disclosed.

85. If the boards of directors of pooling cooperatives do not assign amounts that approximate market to unprocessed products received from patrons, the cooperatives should account for inventories at net realizable value (an example is provided in the appendix, column C). Because amounts that approximate estimated market are not assigned to products received from patrons, cost of goods sold will not include a charge for unprocessed products under this method.

86. Pooling cooperatives should not use the cash advance method to account for inventories.

Accounting for Investments in and Income From Cooperatives

87. Member patrons of cooperatives can be producers or other cooperatives. Member patrons provide most of the capital required by cooperatives. The capital usually represents long-term investments acquired through initial cash investments, retains, or noncash patronage allocations. Voting rights for those investments are usually based on one-member-one-vote or limited weighted voting rather than on the number or amount of securities or other evidence of equity ownership held. The investments are made primarily to obtain an economical source of supply or marketing services and not on the expectation of a return on investment. The sale of such investments, other than back to the issuing cooperative, is usually restricted or prohibited.

Diversity in Practice

88. Investments in cooperatives are generally carried by producers at cost, at cost plus declared retains, at cost plus estimated retains, or at an amount less than cost.

89. Most cooperatives carry their investments in other cooperatives at cost if they are purchased or at face amount if they are received in other than purchase transactions (retains or noncash patronage allocations). However, they usually write the investments down to estimated net realizable value if evidence indicates they will be unable to recover the full carrying amount of the investments. That practice has been endorsed in Accounting Research Bulletin 2, issued by the National Society of Accountants for Cooperatives, which states—

> Investments in cooperatives made by user patrons for the purpose of providing capital for operations of the investee cooperative should be carried at cost, if purchased, or at face value if received in transactions other than purchases such as non-cash patronage dividends. Such investments should be written down to an appropriate amount if reliable evidence indicates that their value has been permanently impaired.

> It should be noted that in most instances accounting for investments in other cooperatives (including banks for cooperatives and other cooperative financing organizations, such as the National Rural Utilities Cooperative Finance Corporation) on the basis outlined above results in investment carrying values equal to the equity values of the investing cooperative's interest in the investee cooperatives; therefore, it would appear that the basis outlined complies with APB Opinion No. 18, *The Equity Method of Accounting for Investments in Common Stock*, to the extent that the intent of the opinion is applicable to investments of cooperatives. In the infrequent instances where the investor's share of unallocated retained earnings of an investee cooperative is material to the investor, the principles set forth in APB Opinion No. 18 should be applied.

90. Cooperatives that invest in other cooperatives usually recognize allocated equities in the cooperative investor's fiscal year within which written notice of allocation is received, and the investment is carried at cost plus allocated equities. That method of revenue recognition conforms with federal income tax requirements. It is the most practical method of reporting because many investee cooperatives issue financial statements and determine patronage allocations only at the close of their accounting years. Many cooperatives do that because they find determination of patronage allocations to be complex and time consuming, since their operations may include both marketing and supply functions, as well as several departments under each function.

91. Diversity in practice has developed in accounting for unallocated equities. Some patrons who hold at least a 20 percent ownership interest recognize their interest in unallocated equities in accordance with APB Opinion No. 18. Others do not recognize unallocated equities, primarily because the equity ownership percentage changes according to patronage and because voting is usually based on the one-member-one-vote principle, which does not necessarily provide significant influence. Interpretation and application of APB Opinion No. 18 may become more significant in financial reporting for cooperatives because 1978 changes in the Internal Revenue Code, relating to the investment tax credit, may encourage cooperatives to reduce distributions of assets to patrons and increase unallocated net after-tax earnings for the purchase of assets.

92. Most patrons recognize their patronage allocations when they are notified, which conforms with federal income tax reporting requirements. Other patrons accrue patronage allocations on the basis of the cooperatives' interim financial statements.

93. Presentation of patronage allocations in patrons' financial statements is also diverse. Some patrons recognize patronage allocations as reductions of purchase or interest costs on purchases from supply or financing cooperatives or as increases in sales for deliveries to marketing cooperatives. Other patrons recognize all patronage allocations as nonoperating income.

Authoritative Literature

94. Authoritative literature on marketable investments—Statement of Financial Accounting Standards No. 12,[*] *Accounting for Certain Marketable Securities*, and FASB Interpretation No. 16, *Clarification of Definitions and Accounting for Marketable Equity Securities That Become Nonmarketable*—has little applicability to investments in cooperatives. Investments in cooperatives are not equity securities and usually are not readily marketable, and transfer or sale, other than back to the issuing cooperative, is usually restricted or prohibited. Current accounting literature supports the carrying of long-term investments, such as nonmarketable investments in agricultural cooperatives, at cost if the value of the investments is not impaired. Carrying amounts are reduced when the investor becomes unable to recover the full carrying amounts. APB Opinion No. 18 requires the equity method of accounting for investments in which the investor has significant influence over an investee's operating and financial policies.

95. The significance of investments by patrons results primarily from the purchasing or marketing rights and participation in the operating earnings. As such, the operations of cooperatives have many of the attributes of corporate joint ventures or partnerships.

Pros and Cons

96. Some accountants argue that the investment in a cooperative is in substance a long-term investment and, as such, should be carried at cost or at cost plus allocated equities. Others believe that the investments should be

---

[*] FASB Statement No. 115, *Accounting for Certain Investments in Debt and Equity Securities*, supersedes FASB Statement No. 12.

discounted to their present value. The carrying amounts would be adjusted downward as required by generally accepted accounting principles when the patron becomes unable to recover the full carrying amounts.

97. Those that support discounting of investments in cooperatives to present value believe that it results in satisfactory presentation in the financial statements because allocated equities are usually not redeemed or are redeemed over a long period. However, others believe that patrons contribute amounts to cooperatives not as investments but to obtain supply or marketing sources, and the allocated equities represent a proportionate share of the cooperative's earnings for the period of patronage. That is similar to accounting for equities in partnerships or corporate joint ventures, in which undistributed earnings are recognized for accounting purposes on the same basis as for federal income tax reporting. Proponents of the stated amount method also believe that it produces symmetry, since the investee records the issuance of securities or book credits at par or face amounts rather than on the basis of discounted values. They argue further that the method conforms with the underlying price-adjustment theory of cooperatives, which holds that such allocated equities are merely reductions of the cost of supply purchases or increases in the proceeds of products marketed through the cooperative and that they should therefore be reflected in the patrons' results of operations.

98. Accountants who believe that a cooperative's unallocated losses should not be recognized by the patrons base their contention on the premise that operating losses may indicate temporary rather than permanent declines in value because they may result from identifiable, isolated, or nonrecurring events. Accordingly, they should not be recognized. Furthermore, because many investor cooperatives determine patronage allocations on the basis of financial statement reporting rather than federal income tax reporting, some accountants argue that financial statement recognition by investor cooperatives of unallocated losses will cause the payment of federal income taxes by the investor cooperative that would not otherwise be payable and such taxes will not be recoverable if the losses are later allocated. That adverse effect is the result of federal income tax regulations that limit the patronage refund deduction to the lesser of the patronage refund "paid" and the patronage refund "allowable," as determined in accordance with federal income tax rules and regulations.

99. Those who believe that unallocated losses should be recognized argue that patrons must recognize allocated losses for consistent reporting, much as if the investment were in a corporate joint venture or partnership rather than a cooperative. They further contend that failure to recognize unallocated losses permits manipulation of earnings because patrons often serve on the cooperative's board of directors or can influence the board of directors, which has the authority to determine the portions, if any, of the losses that will be allocated to patrons.

100. Accountants who believe that unallocated equities should not be recognized by the patrons generally contend that APB Opinion No. 18 does not apply because equity ownership generally does not convey voting control and because ownership interests in unallocated equities may be temporary, being subject to changes in patronage participation and the redemption of equities. However, others argue that APB Opinion No. 18 should apply to all investments in cooperatives in which the patrons hold at least 20 percent of the equity securities, regardless of the one-member-one-vote requirement and the fact that ownership interests may change. They believe that the patron frequently has significant influence due to patronage volume, assured representation on the board of directors, or other means.

101. Some accountants believe that patronage allocations should be recognized in the accounting period in which the supply is purchased or the product is marketed, since those transactions are the source of the patronage allocations and are adjustments of the price at which the supply is purchased or the product marketed. Others believe that the accrual of estimated patronage allocations is impractical because many cooperatives do not determine patronage allocations during interim periods and the amount of the allocations usually cannot be determined from the cooperatives' interim financial statements. Further, existing federal income tax rules and regulations, as well as the bylaws of most investee cooperatives, require the investee's patronage allocations to be included in taxable income in the period the investor is notified of the patronage allocation. This requirement may cause adverse tax effects for investors.

102. Some accountants argue that allocated and unallocated equities should be reflected in the statement of operations as reductions of costs or increases in proceeds because such amounts result from the transactions by which supplies are purchased, interest is paid, or products are sold. Accordingly, the proponents believe that the equities should be reported in the same manner as the original transactions to report sales, cost of sales, and operating expenses. Other accountants believe that the allocations should be reported as other income rather than as increases or decreases in sales, cost of sales, or operating expenses; they argue that including the allocations in sales, cost of sales, or operating expenses could misstate gross profit or expenses.

Division Conclusions

103. Investments in cooperatives should be accounted for at cost, including allocated equities and retains. The carrying amount of an investment in a cooperative should be reduced if the patron is unable to recover the full carrying value of the investment. Losses unallocated by the investee may indicate such an inability, and, at a minimum, the excess of unallocated losses over unallocated equities should be recognized by the patron based on the patron's proportionate share of the total equity of the investee cooperative, or any other appropriate method, unless the patron demonstrates that it is probable that the carrying amount of the investment in the cooperative can be fully recovered.

104. Patrons should recognize patronage refunds either—

a.   When the related patronage occurs if it is then probable that (1) a patronage refund applicable to the period will be declared, (2) one or more future events confirming the receipt of a patronage refund are expected to occur, (3) the amount of the refund can be reasonably estimated, and (4) the accrual can be consistently made from year to year or

b.   On notification by the distributing cooperative.

The accrual should be based on the latest available reliable information and should be adjusted on notification of allocation.

105. Either (1) the classification of the allocations in the financial statements should follow the recording of the costs or proceeds or (2) the allocations should be presented separately.

Effective Date and Transition

106. The Accounting Standards Division recommends application of this statement to financial statements prepared for fiscal years, and interim periods in such fiscal years, beginning after June 15, 1985. Accounting changes to conform to the recommendations of this statement should be made prospectively for transactions or activities occurring on or after the effective date of this statement. Application for earlier years, including retroactive application, is encouraged for all transactions or activities regardless of when they occurred. Disclosures should be made in the financial statements in the period of change in accordance with APB Opinion No. 20, *Accounting Changes.*

APPENDIX

Accounting by Pooling Cooperatives for Products Received From Patrons

The following illustrates the statement of net earnings prepared under each of two possible methods of accounting for inventories (columns A and B), the statement of net proceeds prepared under the net realizable value method (column C), and the respective statements of amounts due patrons, if such latter statement is included in the financial statements. (See paragraphs 83, 84, and 85.) Column A demonstrates the lower of cost or market method with patrons' raw product being charged to cost of production at assigned amounts. Column B demonstrates the net realizable value method with patrons' raw product being charged to cost of production at assigned amounts. Column C demonstrates the net realizable value method when no amounts are assigned to patrons' raw product; therefore, there is no charge to cost of production for patrons' raw product. The assumed facts are as follows:

Sales	$129,630
Beginning inventory	
Net realizable value	31,128
Lower of cost or market	28,380
Assigned value of patrons' raw product received	56,500
Ending inventory	
Net realizable value	35,596
Lower of cost or market	32,360
Income taxes	1,250
Other costs and expenses	56,580
Amounts paid to patrons, retains, and non- patronage earnings	74,430
Amounts due patrons at beginning of year	
Lower of cost or market method	8,910
Net realizable value method	11,748

Statements of Net Earnings (columns A and B)

Statement of Net Proceeds (column C)

	Inventories Valued At		
	Lower of Cost or Market—A	Net Realizable Value—B	Net Realizable Value—C
Sales	$129,630	$129,630	$129,630
Costs and expenses (I)	109,100	108,702	52,202
Earnings before income taxes	20,530	20,928	—
Proceeds before income taxes	—	—	77,428
Income taxes	1,250	1,250	1,250
Net earnings	$ 19,280	$ 19,678	
Net proceeds			$ 76,178
I. Beginning inventory	$ 28,380	$ 31,218	$ 31,218
Assigned value of patrons' raw product received	56,500	56,500	—
Ending inventory	(32,360)	(35,596)	(35,596)
Other costs and expenses	56,580	56,580	56,580
	$109,100	$108,702	$ 52,202

Statements of Amounts Due Patrons

	Inventories Valued At		
	Lower of Cost or Market—A	Net Realizable Value—B	Net Realizable Value—C
Amounts due patrons at beginning of year ·	$ 8,910	$11,748	$11,748
Net earnings	19,280	19,678	—
Net proceeds	—	—	76,178
Assigned value of patrons' raw product received	56,500	56,500	—
	84,690	87,926	87,926
Less amounts paid to patrons, retains, and non-patronage earnings	74,430	74,430	74,430
Amounts due patrons at end of year	$10,260	$13,496	$13,496

Under the two inventory methods presented, the difference in amounts due patrons at the end of the year results from the difference in the ending inventory valuations, illustrated as follows:

Inventories of finished goods and goods in process at:	
Net realizable value	$35,596
Lower of cost or market	(32,360)
	3,236
Amounts due patrons at end of year on lower of cost or market basis	10,260
Amounts due patrons at end of year on net realizable value basis	$13,496

Appendix D

Information Sources

Further information on matters addressed in this Guide is available through various publications and services listed in the table that follows. Many non-government and some government publications and services involve a charge or membership requirement.

Fax services allow users to follow voice cues and request that selected documents be sent by fax machine. Some fax services require the user to call from the handset of the fax machine, others allow the user to call from any phone. Most fax services offer an index document, which lists titles and other information describing available documents.

Recorded announcements allow users to listen to announcements about a variety of recent or scheduled actions or meetings.

All telephone numbers listed are voice lines, unless otherwise designated as fax (f) lines.

Information Sources

Organization	General Information	Fax/Phone Services	Internet Web Site	Recorded Announcements
American Institute of Certified Public Accountants	*Order Department* Harborside Financial Center 201 Plaza Three Jersey City, NJ 07311-3881 (888) 777-7077	*24 Hour Fax Hotline* (201) 938-3787	http://www.aicpa.org	
Financial Accounting Standards Board	*Order Department* P.O. Box 5116 Norwalk, CT 06856-5116 (203) 847-0700, ext. 10		http://www.fasb.org	*Action Alert Telephone Line* (203) 847-0700 (ext. 444)
U.S. General Accounting Office	*Superintendent of Documents* U.S. Government Printing Office Washington, DC 20401-0001 (202) 512-1800 (202) 512-2250 (f)		*U.S. Government Printing Office's The Federal Bulletin Board* Includes *Federal Register* notices and the Code of Federal Regulations. Users are usually expected to open a deposit account. User assistance line: (202) 512-1530 www.access.gpo.gov/su_docs/index.html	
U.S. Department of Agriculture	14th & Independence Ave., SW Washington, DC 20250 (202) 720-2791		http://www.usda.gov	
U.S. Securities and Exchange Commission	*Publications Unit* 450 Fifth Street, NW Washington, DC 20549-0001 (202) 942-4040 *SEC Public Reference Room* (202) 942-8090	*Information Line* (202) 942-8088, ext. 4 (202) 942-7114 (tty)	http://www.sec.gov	*Information Line* (202) 942-8088 (202) 942-7114 (tty)
Farm Financial Standards Council	Carroll Merry Farm Financial Standards Council 1212 South Naper Blvd., Ste. 119 Naperville, IL 60540 (630) 637-0199		http://www.ffsc.org	

Appendix E

Schedule of Changes Made to Agricultural Producers and Agricultural Cooperatives

As of May 2004

Beginning May 2001, all schedules of changes reflect only current year activity to improve clarity.

Reference	Change
General	Deleted "Audits of" in all references to all applicable Guide titles.
Preface	Updated to reflect the applicability and requirements of the Sarbanes-Oxley Act, related SEC regulations, and Standards of the PCAOB; Footnote 1 added.
Paragraph 3.01	Footnote * added; Footnote 1 revised to clarify guidance.
Paragraph 3.02 (footnote *)	Added.
Paragraph 3.15	Footnote * deleted.
Chapter 4 (Title)	Revised to reflect transfer of guidance to chapter 12 to eliminate redundancy relating to audit documentation and internal control; Footnote * added.
Paragraphs 4.03, 4.04 (and footnote 1), 4.05 (and footnote 2), 4.06 (and footnote 3), and 4.07	Deleted and transferred to new paragraphs 12.22, 12.23 (and footnote 4), 12.24 (and footnote 5), 12.25 (and footnote 6), and 12.26.
Paragraphs 4.08, 4.09 (and footnote 4), 4.10 (and footnotes 5 and 6), 4.11, 4.12, 4.13, 4.14, 4.15, 4.16, 4.17, and 4.18	Deleted and transferred to new paragraphs 12.28, 12.29, 12.30 (and footnote 7), 12.31 (and footnotes 8 and 9), 12.32, 12.33, 12.34, 12.35, 12.36, 12.37, 12.38, 12.39, 12.40, 12.41, 12.42, and 12.43.
Chapter 6 (Title)	Revised to clarify guidance; Footnote * added.
Paragraphs 6.25, 6.33, 6.47, and 6.55 (footnotes *)	Deleted.
Paragraph 6.56 (footnote **)	Redesignated as footnote *.
Paragraphs 6.60 and 6.69 (and footnote 1)	Revised to clarify guidance.

Reference	Change
Paragraph 6.74 (footnote **)	Deleted.
Paragraph 6.77	Revised to clarify guidance.
Paragraph 6.80	Added to reflect the issuance of FASB Interpretation No. 46 (revised December 2003); Subsequent paragraphs renumbered.
Renumbered paragraph 6.81	Revised to reflect the issuance of the Audit Guide *Auditing Derivative Instruments, Hedging Activities, and Investments in Securities*; Footnote 2 deleted; Subsequent footnote renumbered.
Former paragraph 6.103 (and footnote 3)	Deleted.
Paragraph 7.05 (footnote *)	Added.
Paragraph 8.08	Revised to add discussion about revolvement practices especially the role of board discretion; Footnote * added.
Chapter 9 (Title)	Revised to reflect transfer of guidance to chapter 12 to eliminate redundancy relating to audit documentation and internal control; Footnote * added.
Paragraph 9.01	Revised to clarify guidance; Footnote ** added.
Paragraphs 9.02, 9.03 (and footnote 1), 9.04 (and footnote 2), 9.05 (and footnote 3), and 9.06	Deleted and transferred to new paragraphs 12.22, 12.23 (and footnote 4), 12.24 (and footnote 5), 12.25 (and footnote 6), and 12.26.
Paragraphs 9.07, 9.08 (and footnote 4), 9.09 (and footnotes 5 and 6), 9.10, 9.11, 9.12, 9.13, 9.14, 9.15, 9.16, and 9.17	Deleted and transferred to new paragraphs 12.28, 12.29, 12.30 (and footnote 7), 12.31 (and footnotes 8 and 9), 12.32, 12.33, 12.34, 12.35, 12.36, 12.37, 12.38, 12.39, 12.40, 12.41, 12.42, and 12.43.
Chapter 10 (Title)	Footnote * revised; Footnote ** added.
Chapter 11 (Title) and paragraph 11.09 (footnotes *)	Added.
Paragraph 11.18	Added to reflect the issuance of FASB Interpretation No. 46 (revised December 2003); Subsequent paragraphs renumbered.
Renumbered paragraph 11.19	Revised to reflect the issuance of the Audit Guide *Auditing Derivative Instruments, Hedging Activities, and Investments in Securities*.

Reference	Change
Renumbered paragraph 11.23 (footnote *)	Added.
Renumbered paragraph 11.29	Revised to add discussion about revolvement practices.
Former paragraph 11.39 (and footnote 1)	Deleted.
Chapter 12 (Title)	Revised to reflect transfer of guidance related to audit documentation, internal control, auditing fair value measurements and disclosures, asset retirement obligations, and consolidation of variable interest entities from chapters 4, 9, and 11; Footnote * added.
Paragraph 12.01 (heading)	Added to clarify guidance.
Paragraph 12.15	Added to provide discussion on interest rate swaps; Subsequent paragraphs renumbered.
Renumbered paragraph 12.16	Revised to clarify guidance and to reflect the issuance of FASB Statement No. 149; Footnote 1 deleted; Subsequent footnotes renumbered.
Renumbered paragraph 12.17 (renumbered footnote 1)	Revised to clarify guidance.
Renumbered paragraph 12.18 (former footnote 3)	Deleted.
Paragraph 12.19 (and footnote 2)	Transferred from former paragraphs 6.103 (and footnote 3) and 11.39 (and footnote 1).
Paragraphs 12.20 (and footnotes * and 3) and 12.21	Added to reflect the issuance of FASB Interpretation No. 46 (revised December 2003).
Paragraphs 12.22, 12.23 (and footnote 4), 12.24 (and footnote 5), 12.25 (and footnote 6), and 12.26	Transferred from former paragraphs 4.03, 4.04 (and footnote 1), 4.05 (and footnote 2), 4.06 (and footnote 3), 4.07, 9.02, 9.03 (and footnote 1), 9.04 (and footnote 2), 9.05 (and footnote 3), 9.06, and 9.07; Footnote * added.
Paragraph 12.27	Added to alert readers about the SEC rule Retention of Records Relevant to Audits and Reviews.
Paragraphs 13.22 and 13.30 (footnotes *)	Added.
Paragraph 13.33c	Revised to clarify guidance.

Reference	Change
Appendix B	Illustrative Financial Statements of an Agricultural Producer: Revised to reflect the issuance of FASB Statements No. 137, No. 138, and No. 149; Footnotes * and ** added; Independent Auditor's Report: Revised to clarify guidance; Footnote * added; Exhibit B-3: Grain and Cattle Producer, Inc. Note 1: Footnote * deleted; Note 3: Footnote * deleted; Footnote 2 revised to delete and transfer SAS No. 101 guidance into new paragraphs 12.40, 12.41, 12.42, and 12.43; Note 6: Footnote 3 revised to reflect the issuance of FASB Statement No. 149; Footnote 4 revised to delete and transfer SAS No. 101 guidance into new paragraphs 12.40, 12.41, 12.42, and 12.43; Exhibit B-5: Illustrative Financial Statements of Agricultural Cooperatives: Footnotes *, **, and † added; Exhibits B-6, B-8, and B-9: Midstate Marketing Cooperative Balance Sheets, Statements of Amounts Due to Patrons, and Statements of Patrons' Equities, respectively: Footnotes * added; Exhibit B-10: Midstate Marketing Cooperative Note 1: Footnote * replaced; Note 4: Footnote * added; Note 6: Footnote 10 revised to reflect the issuance of FASB Statement No. 149; Footnote 11 revised to delete and transfer SAS No. 101 guidance into new paragraphs 12.40, 12.41, 12.42, and 12.43; Exhibits B-12, B-14, B-15, and B-17: Midstate Marketing Cooperative Statements of Amounts Due to Patrons, Central Supply Cooperative Balance Sheets, and Statements of Patrons' Equities, respectively: Footnote * added; Exhibit B-18: Central Supply Cooperative Note 1: Footnote * deleted; Footnotes * and ** added; Note 4: Footnote * added; Note 7: Footnote 16 revised to reflect the issuance of FASB Statement No. 149; Footnote 17 revised to delete and transfer SAS No. 101 guidance into new paragraphs 12.40, 12.41, 12.42, and 12.43.
Glossary (footnotes *)	Added.

Glossary

abnormal costs. Those costs above normal costs (which can be defined as an acceptable standard of achievement under ordinary operating conditions).

advances. Generally used in marketing cooperatives to denote amounts paid to patrons prior to final settlement. For example, amounts paid to patrons on delivery of crops.

agricultural cooperatives, exempt and nonexempt. Cooperatives classified according to their federal income tax status. Both types are permitted to deduct from taxable income the patronage earnings distributed or allocated on a qualified basis to patrons to the extent that the distributions represent earnings of the cooperative derived from business done with or for the patrons. In addition, cooperatives meeting the requirements of Internal Revenue Code section 521 (exempt cooperatives) are permitted to deduct (1) limited amounts paid as dividends on capital stock and (2) distributions to patrons of income from business done with the U.S. government or its agencies as well as income from nonpatronage sources.

annual. A crop that completes its life cycle, from seed to mature plant, in one growing season.

anticipatory hedge. The use of commodity futures contracts or options to minimize risk from price fluctuations for an expected transaction. For example, a producer who is committed to growing a crop or raising livestock and wishes to fix the sales price may use an anticipatory hedge. Anticipatory hedges are sometimes referred to as forecasted transactions. As defined in FASB Statement No. 133, a forecasted transaction is a transaction that is expected to occur for which there is no firm commitment. Because no transaction or event has yet occurred and the transaction or event when it occurs will be at the prevailing market price, a forecasted transaction does not give an entity any present rights to future benefits or a present obligation for future sacrifices.

assigned amounts. Amounts used to record products delivered by patrons of a marketing cooperative operating on a pooling basis, and the related liability to patrons, if the ultimate amounts to be paid patrons are determined when the pool is closed. These amounts may be established on the basis of current prices paid by other buyers (sometimes referred to as *field prices*), or they may be assigned by the cooperative's board of directors. The assigned amounts are sometimes referred to as *established values*.

base capital plan, revolving capital plan.* Plans designed to require capital investment by cooperative members in proportion to each member's

---

* In May 2003, the FASB issued FASB Statement of Financial Accounting Standards No. 150, *Accounting for Certain Financial Instruments With Characteristics of Both Liabilities and Equity.* This Statement establishes standards for how an issuer classifies and measures certain financial instruments with characteristics of both liabilities and equity. It requires that an issuer classify a financial instrument that is within its scope as a liability (or an asset in some circumstances). Many of those instruments were previously classified as equity.

This Standard may have a significant impact on financial statements of agricultural cooperatives. Retained allocated equities, including retained patronage allocations and per-unit retains, which are usually repaid to cooperative patrons over a specific number of years generally meet the definition of mandatorily redeemable financial instruments under FASB Statement No. 150 and as such may have to be reclassified as liabilities. As a result, some agricultural cooperatives may report significantly reduced equities and increased liabilities in their GAAP financial statements.

In November 2003, the FASB issued FASB Staff Position (FSP) FAS 150-3, which defers the effective date of the mandatorily redeemable provisions of FASB Statement No. 150 and all related FSPs for nonpublic entities as follows: (*a*) until fiscal periods beginning after December 15, 2004 for instruments that are mandatorily redeemable on fixed dates and (*b*) indefinitely, pending further FASB action, if the redemption date is not fixed or if the payout amount is variable and not based on an index. Readers should be alert to further developments.

current use of the cooperative. A base capital plan is usually funded over a specific period of time with an established amount of investment required each year. Capital investment is evidenced by the issuance of capital certificates (qualified or nonqualified written notices of allocation) in lieu of cash payments to members. These certificates are typically redeemed in series according to year of issue, with the earliest years first. The revolving cycle is determined by the board of directors on the basis of current capital requirements.

bed. An area of ground prepared for seeding or planting.

breeding herd. A group of animals used for breeding purposes.

broiler chickens. Chickens produced for slaughter.

capital certificates (revolving fund certificates, capital-retain certificates). [*] A type of patrons' equities withheld by cooperatives from distributions of net earnings, credited to the patron's account, and usually revolved (paid) over a specific number of years.

cash advance method (cost advance method). A method of accounting for inventories of a marketing cooperative operating on a pool basis. Under this method, inventories are accounted for at the amount of cash advances made to patrons.

cash or spot price. The price at which commodities available for immediate delivery are currently selling.

commercial herd. A breeding herd used to produce standard-quality animals without emphasis on any particular breed or bloodlines.

commercial production. The point at which production from an orchard, vineyard, or grove first reaches a level that makes operations economically feasible based on prices normally expected to prevail.

commodity. An agricultural product, such as wheat or sugar.

consent. Refers to the patron's agreement to report noncash distributions from cooperatives for income tax purposes. Consents are required in order for the cooperative to deduct patronage distributions for income tax purposes.

cover. The purchase (or sale) of a futures contract for a particular commodity to offset a previously established short (or long) position.

crop. Grains, vegetables, fruits, berries, nuts, and fibers grown by agricultural producers. The term is also used to refer to a calf crop.

crop development costs. Costs incurred up to the time crops begin to be produced in commercial quantities, including the costs of land preparation, plants, planting, fertilization, grafting, pruning, equipment use, and irrigation.

crop year. Generally the period from the harvest of a crop to the corresponding period in the following year. When used in connection with commodity markets, the term assumes a more specific meaning. For example, the U.S. crop year for wheat begins on July 1 and for cotton begins on August 1.

crossbreed. An animal that is the product of two different breeds. Sometimes used to denote generations, as in first cross, second cross, and so on.

cross hedge. The use of a commodity traded on a commodity futures market to hedge a commodity for which there is no such market. The practice is acceptable if there is a clear economic relationship between the two commodities, such as when the futures price of the substitute commodity moves in tandem with the cash price of the commodity being hedged, and provided high correlation is probable.

---

[*] See footnote * to *base capital plan, revolving capital plan.*

deep-ripping. To split open the ground in a field at a depth greater than normal plowing so that air, water, and chemicals can penetrate.

feeder. A young animal cared for and fed for a period of time and ultimately destined for slaughter.

feedlot. The enclosed area in which animals are cared for and fed until fattened and ready for slaughter.

forward purchase contract. An agreement to buy production from a specified acreage or to buy a specified quantity of a commodity at a set or determinable price for delivery at a specified future date.

forward sales contract. An agreement to sell production from a specified acreage or to sell a specified quantity of a commodity at a set or determinable price for delivery at a specified future date.

fumigation. To destroy insects by application of smoke, a chemical, or gas vapor. It can be applied to produce in storage. It also includes treatment of soil, often to considerable depth, to kill diseases, nematodes, or viruses.

futures contract. A standard and transferable form of contract that binds the seller to deliver to the bearer a standard amount and grade of a commodity at a specific location at a specified time. It usually includes a schedule of premiums and discounts for quality variation.

futures market. A federally designated commodity exchange organized to provide the facilities and rules for trading certain commodities swiftly and economically, by using uniform contracts for delivery or receipt of commodities of a specified grade at a specified time.

grade. The classification of a commodity or an animal by quality, size, or ripeness. Standards of uniformity are usually designated by a governing group, such as the U.S. Department of Agriculture or a recognized trade association.

grafting. Inserting a living portion of a plant into the limb or trunk of another tree or vine to change the variety of species.

grove. Fruit or nut trees planted in geometric patterns to economically facilitate care of the trees and harvest of the fruit or nuts.

growing crop. A field, row, tree, bush, or vine crop before harvest.

harvested crop. An agricultural product, gathered but unsold.

hatching eggs. Eggs used for production of poultry. Hatching eggs, as distinguished from market eggs, must be fertile.

hedge. Any action taken to reduce the risk of loss from price fluctuations of products to be sold or materials to be purchased. A hedge may be accomplished by the use of forward or commodity futures contracts. As used in this guide, the words *hedge* and *hedging* pertain to the use of commodity futures contracts and options bought and sold on established markets.

hedging-procedures method. A method of accounting for inventory, commonly used by grain merchants, in which the approximate cost of hedged inventories is determined by pricing quantities on hand at market and by adjusting for gains and losses on related open futures and forward contracts.

hybrid. Any new or different variety of animal, plant, tree, or vine produced by crossbreeding or pollinizing two or more varieties within a general species.

livestock. Registered and commercial cattle, sheep, hogs, horses, poultry, and small animals bred and raised by agricultural producers.

mark-to-market. A method of accounting for inventories, forward contracts, options and futures contracts at current market prices and of recognizing changes in market prices as gains and losses.

market-order prices. Prices for raw products established by federal or state agencies.

marketing cooperative. A cooperative that markets the products (crops, livestock, and so on) produced by its patrons.

marketing pool. A method of accounting for business done between patrons and their marketing cooperative whereby the cooperative usually takes title to the raw product on delivery, commingles products of like kind and quality, performs whatever processing and packaging are required, sells the finished product, and maintains records of sales and payments for product and expenses. When the pool is closed, the cooperative distributes net earnings, less previous advances, to the pool patrons on the basis of the amount or value of product delivered.

member and nonmember (of a cooperative). A member is an owner-patron of a cooperative who is entitled to vote at corporate meetings. A nonmember patron is not entitled to voting privileges. A nonmember patron may or may not be entitled to share in patronage distributions, depending on the articles and bylaws of the cooperative or on other agreements.

net inventory position. The quantity of a specified commodity on hand that is adjusted for the quantities on open forward and futures contracts.

net proceeds, net margins, net savings, net earnings. Used to denote the excess of marketing or sales proceeds over costs of operations and income taxes. They normally represent the amount available for distribution to patrons on a patronage basis.

net realizable value. Valuation of inventories at estimated selling prices in the ordinary course of business, less reasonably predictable costs of completion, disposal, and transportation.

nonpatronage income. Earnings other than those from business done with or for patrons on a patronage basis.

nonqualified written notice of allocation. A nonqualified written notice of allocation is similar to a qualified written notice of allocation, except that no portion of the nonqualified notice is paid in cash at the time of notification and the patron is not required to report it for income tax purposes until redemption.

normal costs. Those costs that conform to an acceptable standard of achievement under ordinary operating conditions.

open contract. An unliquidated (or open) futures contract.

option. A contract allowing, but not requiring, its holder to buy (call) or sell (put) a specific or standard commodity or financial or equity instrument at a specified price during a specified time period. The principal difference between an option and a futures contract is that the exercise of a futures contract is mandatory.

orchard (see grove). Fruit trees planted in geometric patterns to economically facilitate care of the trees and harvest of the fruit.

patron. Any individual, trust, estate, partnership, corporation, or cooperative with whom or for whom a cooperative does business on a cooperative basis, whether a member or nonmember of the cooperative association.

patronage. The amount of business done with a cooperative by one of its patrons. Patronage is measured by either the quantity or value of commodities received from patrons by a marketing cooperative and the quantity or value of the goods and services sold to patrons by a supply cooperative.

patronage allocations.[*] Patronage earnings distributed, or allocated, to individual patrons on the basis of each patron's proportionate share of total patronage. Such allocations, which include notification to the patron, may be made on a qualified or nonqualified basis.

patronage earnings.[*] The excess of a cooperative's revenues over its costs arising from transactions done with or for its patrons. Generally, a significant portion of those earnings is allocated to the cooperative's patrons in the form of cash, allocated equities, or both.

patron equities.[*] Funds invested by the members of a cooperative, in the form of either cash or reinvested noncash patronage distributions, that represent ownership in the cooperative rather than debt. These investments may be represented by capital stock, membership certificates, capital certificates, patronage certificates, revolving-fund certificates, or other similar instruments.

per-unit retain.[*] A form of financing used by marketing cooperatives and usually based on tonnage or quantities of product delivered by patrons. Typically it involves withholding cash from the amounts advanced to patrons at time of delivery. These withheld amounts are ultimately distributed in the form of written notices of allocation, and they differ from patronage refunds because they are not determined on the basis of net earnings. There is no 20-percent cash payment requirement in order for written notices of allocation to be tax deductible.

per-unit retain certificate. A written notice of allocation to the recipient that states the dollar amount of a per-unit allocation.

pooling cooperative. A marketing cooperative that receives its members' agricultural products without obligation to pay a fixed price and commingles those products into single or multiple pools for processing and marketing purposes. Pool periods may vary from a week to a year or longer, depending on the product involved. Generally profits or losses are allocated to patrons upon closing of the pool.

pools. Accounting control centers used for determining earnings and patronage refunds due to particular patrons.

Open pools are accounting control centers that are not closed (i.e., accounted for) at the end of each accounting period. Open pools are sometimes used by marketing cooperatives for crops that may not be sold for two or more years after their receipt from patrons.

A *single-pool* cooperative determines net proceeds or patronage refunds on the basis of overall operating results for all commodities marketed during an accounting period.

A *multiple-pool* cooperative determines net proceeds or patronage refunds on the basis of separate commodities departments.

---

[*] See footnote * to *base capital plan, revolving capital plan.*

progeny. Offspring of animals or plants.

pruning. Cutting away unwanted portions of trees or vines to shape them and to encourage forms of growth that will enhance production and harvest.

pullet. A hen less than one year old.

qualified check. A check or other instrument redeemable in money that is paid as part of a patronage refund or other payment to a distributee who has not given consent with respect to such patronage refund or payment. Imprinted on the check is a statement explaining that endorsing and cashing the check within ninety days constitutes consent by the payee to include in gross income the dollar amount of the written notice of allocation.

qualified per-unit-retain certificate. Any per-unit-retain certificate that the distributee has agreed to recognize for income tax purposes.

qualified written notice of allocation. A written notice of allocation of a patronage distribution from a cooperative to a patron when the distributee has consented to report the distribution for income tax purposes and the cooperative also distributes a cash payment, or a qualified check, equal to 20 percent or more of the total patronage distribution. The term also includes a written notice of allocation that may be redeemed in full for cash within ninety days of its issuance.

raised animals. Animals produced and raised from an owned herd, as opposed to purchased animals.

recurring land development costs. Costs that do not result in permanent or long-term improvements to land (for example, maintenance costs that occur annually or periodically).

registered herd. Animals with characteristics and genealogical information that make them an established breed, with records maintained for each successive generation.

retained earnings (retained margins, earned surplus, unallocated capital reserves, undistributed margins). These terms refer to unallocated earnings of cooperatives on which income taxes have been paid.

retains.* Amounts determined on a per-unit basis or as a percentage of patronage earnings that are withheld by cooperatives from distributions and allocated to patrons' capital accounts.

revolvement.* A colloquial term referring to a plan for redeeming retained allocated equities previously issued to the cooperative patrons.

rootstock. A variety or type of root used to develop trees, vines, or plants by grafting the rootstock onto a different species or variety to produce a tree or vine with the best attributes of the combined varieties. Different rootstocks are usually used to obtain disease or virus-resistant trees or vines.

speculative contracts. Commodity futures and options contracts entered into without offsetting actual or anticipated ownership of or commitments to purchase or sell the commodity.

stated value. The value assigned to a commodity delivered by patrons that approximates the amount the commodity would have sold for on the open market.

---

* See footnote * to *base capital plan, revolving capital plan.*

summer fallow. The practice of plowing soil so that it will lay open to air and water without the need to support growth for a season.

supply cooperative. A cooperative that supplies to its patrons goods and services used by them in producing their products.

unit-livestock method. Accounting for livestock by using an arbitrary fixed periodic charge. For raised animals the amount is accumulated by periodic increments from birth to maturity or disposition. For purchased animals the arbitrary fixed periodic amount is added to the acquisition cost until maturity or disposition of the animal. The use of this method is inappropriate under generally accepted accounting principles.

vineyard. Grape vines planted in patterns for commercial cultivation and production.

warehouse receipt. A warehouse-issued certificate that lists goods and produce stored and that must be surrendered to receive delivery of the goods. It may be negotiable or nonnegotiable.

written notices of allocation. Any capital stock, revolving-fund certificate, retain certificate, certificate of indebtedness, letter of advice, or other written notice to the recipient that states the dollar amount allocated to the patron by the cooperative and the portion that constitutes a patronage refund.

AICPA RESOURCE: Accounting & Auditing Literature

The AICPA has created a unique online research tool by combining the power and speed of the Web with comprehensive accounting and auditing standards. *AICPA RESOURCE* includes AICPA's and FASB's libraries:

- AICPA Professional Standards
- AICPA Technical Practice Aids
- AICPA's Accounting Trends & Techniques
- AICPA Audit and Accounting Guides
- AICPA Audit Risk Alerts
- FASB Original Pronouncements
- FASB Current Text
- EITF Abstracts
- FASB Implementation Guides
- FASB's Comprehensive Topical Index

Search for pertinent information from both databases by keyword and get the results ranked by relevancy. Print out important *AICPA RESOURCE* segments and integrate the literature into your engagements and financial statements. Available from anywhere you have Internet access, this comprehensive reference library is packed with the A & A guidance you need—and use—the most. Both libraries are updated with the latest standards and conforming changes.

AICPA+FASB reference libraries, one-year individual online subscription
No. ORF-XX
AICPA Member $890.00
Nonmember $1,112.50

AICPA reference library, one-year individual online subscription
No. ORS-XX
AICPA Member $395.00
Nonmember $493.75

AICPA RESOURCE also offers over 50 additional subscription products—log onto www.cpa2biz.com/AICPAresource for details.

For more information or to order, log onto www.cpa2biz.com/AICPAresource, or call 1-888-777-7077.